Your Love Is Blasting in My Heart
A Grandmother's Journey

Marilyn Saltzman

First edition published in 2020
Copyright © by Bubbe Press

All rights reserved.

Inside design by Teresa Ford
Cover design and photography by Hancey Design

ISBN 978-0-578-63823-2

Inspired by
Selamnesh Faith Dusharm
Dian Le Dusharm

Dedicated to
My mother, Rene Schwartz, who taught me
Jewish ethics by living them

Table of Contents

Praise for

Your Love Is Blasting in My Heart
A Grandmother's Journey

"What a sweet and wise book! Jewish tradition defines the wise person as the one who learns from everyone, and the young teachers who share their lessons with their grandmother here work magic to transform the ordinary into the extraordinary and reawaken a sense of joyful wonder in the reader's heart. With the clarity only available to a young mind they inspire us to open our eyes wide to see afresh God's handiwork in our world. Every page delivers delights of humor, joy, hope and inspiration for the journey of life we are all on."
— Alan Morinis, founder of The Mussar Institute
and author of *Everyday Holiness*

"*Your Love Is Blasting In My Heart* is a highly readable, honest and open-hearted celebration of the grandparent-grandchild relationship. Marilyn vividly demonstrates how being an engaged grandparent can be a spiritual practice. Drawing on her many years of *Mussar* experience, Marilyn shows us how this ancient Jewish practice of spiritual and character development can help grandparents become more compassionate, humble, patient and courageous allies to their children and grandchildren. Contemporary research demonstrates the central role grandparents can play in transmitting Jewish identity and values to their grandchildren. This book is a guide for grandparents who want to take up this sacred charge."
— Rabbi David Jaffe, author of *Changing the World from the Inside Out:*
A Jewish Approach to Personal and Social Change,
winner of the National Jewish Book Award

"Marilyn Saltzman has written a wonderful addition to the growing collection of modern and accessible *Mussar* books. This engaging and

inspiring book makes Jewish teachings relevant to everyday life."
— Greg Marcus, author of *The Spiritual Practice of Good Actions: Finding Balance Through the Soul Traits of Mussar*

"Marilyn Saltzman has written a wise and intimate book about the love and work of being a grandmother. Her use of the Jewish traditions of Mussar gives the book richness and texture, but they should not dissuade grandmothers and those with grandmothers of all persuasions to read and savor this book."
— Amy Frykholm, author of *Christian Understandings of the Future: The Historical Trajectory*

"Your Love is Blasting in My Heart is the acutely observed, deeply felt memoir of an American grandmother welcoming, learning with, and loving her two foreign-born, adopted grandchildren. But it is much more than that, as Marilyn Saltzman offers us her family's experiences through the lens of *Mussar*, the Jewish study of attributes. In teaching the reader about *Mussar* while sharing moments with her beloved new family members, Saltzman provides insights that bring us along on her tantalizing voyage of discovery and affection. I heartily recommend this superb book."
— Diane Mott Davidson, *New York Times* bestselling author of the Goldy, the caterer, series

"Drawing on her own experience as a parent and grandparent, Marilyn Saltzman narrates delightful, relatable, intergenerational stories ripe with universal wisdoms we can operationalize in our everyday encounters with one another. These are *bubbe-meisehs* of the highest order. With this book, you too can join the diverse community of souls that has joined her in the effort to cultivate ears that listen with compassion and gratitude, faces that shine with curiosity and joy, hands that lead with generosity and grace, and hearts that blast with love!"
— Rabbi Jamie Arnold, Congregation Beth Evergreen

"There are many books that give grandparents' wisdom to the younger generation. This book, well written, sprightly and deep without being pedantic, uses the actions and expressions of Saltzman's grandkids. She listens to these children and learns from them as they learn from their environment and interactions. Her insights harmonize with her studies of *Mussar*, the Jewish practice that focuses on acting out and bringing to life the virtues we celebrate."

— Joanne Greenberg, author of *I Never Promised You a Rose Garden*

Author's Notes

About *Mussar* — Jewish ethics

Mussar is a Hebrew word appearing in the biblical Book of Proverbs. From the root meaning "to cause to turn or change directions," it is translated as discipline, instruction or moral conduct and provides a path to living an ethical life through study and mindful practice. It is an ancient Jewish tradition, with literature dating back to the eleventh century.

Mussar was a solitary practice until Rabbi Israel Salanter started a movement among Orthodox Jews in nineteenth century Lithuania because he feared that his young male students, while studying the Torah, had lost sight of ethics. Unfortunately, many of the *Mussar* teachers perished during the Holocaust, and the movement almost vanished. In the last two decades *Mussar* has experienced resurgence in the United States, thanks in large part to Alan Morinis, founder of The Mussar Institute.

Mussar practice is rooted in the *middot* (soul traits) — such as patience, gratitude, compassion, humility — that help us grow in service to others. At my synagogue, Congregation Beth Evergreen, in the foothills of Colorado, we choose a soul trait each month to practice communally, and all ages participate, from our preschoolers to our adult *Mussar* class members. We began studying *Mussar* together over a decade ago. The class has made me more mindful of the impacts of my actions on both myself and others, and this book shares my journey.

Why thirteen chapters on *middot*?

On the advice of my rabbi and teacher, Jamie Arnold, I chose to write about thirteen soul traits in this book. That, however, just scratches the surface of *Mussar* study. Thirteen is a significant number in Judaism because in Exodus, Moses learns that there are thirteen attributes of God. The Jewish philosopher Maimonides refers to thirteen principles of the Jewish faith.

Journal prompts

One useful *Mussar* practice is to keep a journal for *chesbon hanefesh*, or accounting of the soul. By journaling, we reflect on how our soul trait practices played out during our day: the choices we made, the struggles we faced, the successes we experienced and the consequences of our actions. I have included a list of questions at the end of each chapter that readers might find useful if they decide to write about their personal experiences with the soul traits.

The Main Characters

Moo — my nickname

Irv (Poo) — my husband, the grandpa

Dian (DEE-on) — my adopted grandson, born February 2010

Selam, Selamnesh, "you are peace" (Suh-LAHM, Suh-LAHM-nesh) — my adopted granddaughter, born June 2009

Heidi — my adult daughter, mother of Selam and Dian

Robin — my son-in-law, father of Selam and Dian

Kevin — my adult son

Sampa — nickname of my mother, Rene Schwartz

Note: Names of children in Dian's and Selam's classes at school have been changed to honor their privacy.

Preface

Meditation was never my forte. I was much more comfortable in conversation, action, movement. Yet one afternoon, I decide to take a risk and participate in a group meditation exercise. Eyes closed, breathing deeply, I tried to relax in one of the royal blue upholstered chairs in the synagogue social hall as Rabbi Jamie Arnold led a dozen of us in guided meditation.

The exercise was the start of a *Mussar* class, and I was wary of both the meditation and the learning. Even though I was born and raised a Jew, I knew nothing about the topic or where this class would take me. On the other hand, I loved learning from Rabbi Arnold, spiritual leader of Congregation Beth Evergreen. Attending this Thursday afternoon class was a way to study something new with a teacher I respected. So I sat silently, unmoving, enjoying the sensation of the sun warming my back through the large glass windows as I attempted to be present and open to learning.

Relaxing in a place of worship was as foreign as the Hebrew words chanted in the synagogue of my youth. The first-born daughter of conservative Jews, I spent many long *Shabbat* mornings as a preteen sandwiched between my father and grandfather in the intimidating synagogue sanctuary in Brooklyn, parroting words I did not understand. Dressed in my best pink plaid dress with its stiff crinoline, I sat on a long wooden bench near the front of the sanctuary, crammed in a row of stern-looking men wearing dark suits, white shirts and striped ties. The aged rabbi appeared to be miles away on the raised *bema* with the ornately carved wooden ark whose doors, when opened during the service, revealed the blue-velvet encased Torah scrolls capped with majestic silver crowns.

My father beamed as I learned to sound out the Hebrew words in the worn, leather-covered prayer book. Success! After all, I wasn't looking for a spiritual experience; attending services was a way to get the rarely bestowed approval of my father, ordinarily quicker to anger than to praise.

As I grew older, attending synagogue became a social event. My friends, wearing their new pastel dresses purchased especially for the High Holy Days from Macy's or Abraham & Straus, sat primly outside on the stone stairway and chatted. We sprang into action when the herd of teenage boys sprinted down the steps as they escaped the stifling sanctuary to chase us up and down Remsen Avenue. They swatted us with the white hankies drawn from their suit pockets and tied into knots.

As I progressed through high school, my attendance at synagogue declined, and I quickly forgot the paltry Hebrew I had learned. Yet the traditions and values of Judaism were alive in our home. My mother kept a kosher kitchen; there were separate dishes for meat and dairy; no pork or shellfish ever graced our dining room table; we never drank milk after a meat meal. My mother lit *Shabbat* candles every Friday night. Aunts, uncles and cousins gathered around our Passover table and Chanukah *menorah*.

I grew up and married a Jew, but we shed our religion along with the other stifling cloaks of our New York upbringing when we escaped across the country to Colorado. Yes, we celebrated Passover and Chanukah. We invited friends to a modified, modernized *seder*. Since we were one of only a handful of Jewish families in our mountain community, I brought *dreidels* and a *menorah* to my kids' Scout meetings to counterbalance Santa and Christmas trees. But our attendance at synagogue was spotty. It took decades before we found a comfortable place to call our spiritual home — Congregation Beth Evergreen. The other members were like us, transplanted Jews who had rejected the austere, institutional religion of our parents and sought spiritual and social fulfillment in a more open-minded setting.

Attending the *Mussar* class was a new step in my spiritual journey. Though it is mentioned often in the Bible and scholars wrote about it as early as medieval times, I had never heard the word *Mussar* in my home or synagogue. Because it had almost vanished after World War II when many of the movement's sages had perished, *Mussar*, defined as discipline with instructions on how to live an ethical life, was just now experiencing resurgence.

So it was with curiosity and complete lack of knowledge that I purchased Alan Morinis' book *Everyday Holiness* and began attending Rabbi Arnold's Thursday afternoon *Mussar* classes. We sat around the wobbly, gray plastic tables in the synagogue social hall and began with the prayer for study. Often Rabbi hummed a melody or sang a song before we got started. Other times we meditated or wrote in our journals. We began our learning with the purposes and definitions of *Mussar* in Morinis' book. We talked about how each of us is on a personal spiritual journey that no one else could define for us; that we each had our own work to do on the *middot* of the month, such as patience, humility, gratitude, compassion and generosity.

I was hooked. What if I could become more patient, for example, with my family, friends and even strangers? After years of waiting with annoyance for my husband, Irv, to be ready for breakfast, what if I could just enjoy watching him create his artistic mixture of cereal and five kinds of fruit instead of gobbling down my hard-boiled egg before he even sat down to eat? An interesting yet challenging idea.

The purpose of *Mussar*, I learned, was to improve myself, but not just for myself. It wasn't the Jewish version of self-help. "It's about clarifying the inner light and becoming a lamp shedding light in to the world," Morinis says, "to transform behavior in the service of others."

While some behavioral psychology promotes changing your attitude to change your behavior, in *Mussar* we learned to do the opposite — change behavior to change our hearts. Or as Rabbi Arnold advised, "Fake it till you make it."

I quickly discovered that it was not easy work and it was not just about studying. It was about practice, every day in every interaction.

And it took courage — the courage to become a better person in the service of others, to change lifetime patterns of behavior.

Some days I took two steps forward and three back. I'd be patient at breakfast only to be antsy when waiting for my turn at the kitchen sink to clean up.

"Hurry up and get your dishes done. I have a meeting in an hour, and I still need to shower," I'd pester Irv.

And that still happens many years later. The trick, I learned, was not to be too hard on myself, but instead to take every success and every failure as an opportunity to reflect and keep practicing.

I would stand in the grocery line and take a deep breath. I would read the amusing headlines of the tabloids: *Bigfoot Hoax Turns Deadly; Granny Foils Felons with Fistful of Fruit.* And the mixed messages of headlines on the cover of the women's magazines — *How I Secretly Lost 55 Pounds* and *Blueberry Crumble Bars and More.* I learned to play peek-a-boo with the toddler in the adjacent shopping cart. Or I simply remembered I really had nowhere else to be in this moment. Lo and behold, it worked; I became more patient though not right away and definitely not all the time.

As I saw some forward motion, I continued to learn, and more importantly, practice the *Mussar* principles that most resonated with me:

• **Be mindful, aware and in the moment.** "Learning to stay more awake is central to *Mussar* practice," according to Rabbi Ira Stone. In a culture where we are encouraged and rewarded to multi-task, I had become a master. I would read a book while watching television. I would play Sudoku while talking to my mother on the phone. I would perform balancing poses while brushing my teeth.

I took my dog on a walk around the neighborhood every day, yet spent more time planning what I had to do next than noticing the budding wildflowers or admiring the neighbor's new deck. One day, I looked at a gray house around the corner. *Wasn't that house brown last time I passed?* I wasn't sure. *Can I be that distracted and unaware?* To be more present I developed a practice of looking for one new thing each time I walked our well-traveled road.

• **Life is full of** *bechirah* **points,** says *Mussar* master Rabbi Eliyahu Dessler. He notes that each person has unique *bechirah* points based on life experiences and past decisions. When we are aware of the difference between how we may automatically react and what we know is ethical, we have an opportunity for growth. If I became more mindful of my choices in situations that made me impatient, I could respond in a kinder way.

"Why is that guy chatting with the teller when there are five people in line behind him?" I grumbled under my breath to my sister as we waited to cash a check. Visiting our ailing mother from opposite sides of the country, we were impatient to get the bank chore done. Then the elderly man turned to leave, and I recognized the recent widower from my mom's neighborhood. *He's lonely,* I thought. *I could have spent the time in line visiting with my sister, whom I hadn't seen for a year, rather than saying an unkind word that he probably heard.*

It was a *bechirah* point. I could have chosen to be snooty or to be understanding, and I had made the wrong choice. Rather than beating myself up as I would have done in the past, I thought about what I had learned. *I'll make a better choice next time,* I vowed.

• **Bear the burden of the other.** "Real loving kindness is directed toward the person as she is," says Rabbi Rami Shapiro. How could I practice putting myself in the other person's shoes to express compassion, recognizing that I can't truly know what the "other" is feeling or experiencing?

Driving down a steep hill on the interstate at high speed, I glanced down to adjust the radio dial. When I looked up a millisecond later, I was inches from a black sedan moving at a snail's pace. Unable to stop, I sideswiped his car as we both careened down the highway. Fortunately, no one was hurt. We pulled to the side of the road to exchange information.

"Give me your license so you don't run off, and let's drive into Georgetown to report this to the police," the elderly driver demanded.

Shaken by the accident and offended by his lack of trust, I handed over my license and got back into my car with its dented front fender.

What's someone so old doing on the highway driving so slowly in the first place? He doesn't belong on the interstate, and he created a traffic hazard, I thought, shaking with anger and the residual fright of the accident as I followed him into town.

The police arrived at the gas station where we stopped, and in a shaky voice, the man reported what had happened. "My wife and I are on a little road trip around the state. We had stopped at the scenic overlook and just re-entered the highway when we were hit by her speeding car."

I paled. *So that's why they were going so slowly; he hadn't gotten back up to speed after stopping to enjoy the scenery. It wasn't that he was too old and didn't belong on I-70.* I had ruined an elderly couple's vacation by my carelessness; and worse, in my mind I had shifted the blame from my inattention, which was the true cause of the accident. It was a hard lesson in bearing the burden of the other.

• **Judge on the side of merit.** "Give everyone the benefit of the doubt," advises *Pirkei Avot,* a text that details Jewish ethics. A product of New York City, I grew up wary, expecting the worst when a stranger approached. I was hiking in the wooded park with my dog when from behind I heard the crunch of footsteps drawing rapidly closer. I glanced over my shoulder to see a man in jogging shorts advancing toward me. *Should I run, scream or let go of my dog and let him attack the stranger?*

In that instant of decision, I was transported back to a dusky evening in Brooklyn. I was walking home from my friend's house where we had been studying for our seventh grade math final. I was distracted by algebra and an armload of heavy texts. Suddenly I felt hands grab my breasts from behind. As I turned and screamed, dropping my books, I saw a teenage boy race away.

Now in the woods, I froze. The man got closer and I saw he was waving a shiny object above his head.

"Are these your keys? I found them back there on the trail." He gasped, out of breath from his run.

I reached into my jacket pocket; indeed my keys were gone.

"Thank you. You sure made a positive difference in my day." I smiled in gratitude and relief.

The encounter helped me appreciate that I didn't have to let my past experiences color the present and future. Why not assume good intentions rather than always expecting the worst?

As I accepted the principles and started working on the practices of *Mussar*, I became more aware of my choices and behaviors. Before going to bed, I reflected, sometimes in writing and sometimes just mentally, about how well I had practiced my *middah* that day. Had I fumed and honked when someone cut me off on the highway? Did I respond too quickly in anger when a friend said something that triggered me? Or had I shown compassion without judgment or advice when a colleague was facing a difficult situation?

Developing a focus phrase as I practiced a new *middah* each month was another technique that *Mussar* provided. For patience, I used, "what's the rush?" and repeated the phrase silently as I got stuck behind a school bus on the road out of the neighborhood.

Rabbi Shefa Gold writes, "Every spiritual tradition acknowledges that how we begin our day matters. . . When we begin the day in gratefulness, we step on to the path of love." To practice gratitude first thing in the morning, I began silently reciting, "This is the day the Lord has made, rejoice, rejoice in it," (Psalm 118) before getting out of bed.

I found help in another technique, *va'ad*, sharing my practice with *Mussar* partners who listened without judgment. I talked openly about my frustrations with an acquaintance to whom I responded with thoughtless anger at an assumed insult rather than taking the time to consider her intent. My *va'ad* partner listened in silence, bearing witness without comment, and I found insight just by speaking and hearing my own words.

All of these techniques helped me along my *Mussar* journey. I was feeling good about becoming more mindful about my choices, about becoming aware of what caused an unkind reaction, about my interactions with family and friends.

And then a most wonderful event occurred. My daughter, Heidi, and her husband, Robin, adopted two children from foreign lands. Selam came first; she was eighteen months old when she arrived from Ethiopia after her biological mother, Abeba, took her to the orphanage because they were both starving. A couple of months after she arrived, I began babysitting for Selam every Friday. The following year, Heidi and Robin adopted Dian, a thirty-month-old toddler, from China. He joined Selam, Irv and me in our Friday adventures around Denver with curiosity and enthusiasm. We visited the zoo, the aquarium and the Children's Museum. A favorite was Tiny Town, an outdoor museum with replicas of historical structures, just the right size for the kids to peer into the windows of the miniature buildings like the old schoolhouse with its wooden desks and metal chairs.

I loved every minute I spent with these two children from two different countries and cultures. I watched with joy as they came to trust us, to love us and to share their joy of learning English and adapting to their adopted land. And there was an unexpected benefit. Being grandma to Selam and Dian became my greatest opportunity to grow as a *Mussar* practitioner. I began to enrich my practice, not only from trying to be a role model, but even more by learning about the soul traits from them. They are the inspiration for this book.

Courage — *Ametz Lev*

"When we fully set our heart on doing something, our determination can give us the inner strength to overcome fear, doubt and other obstacles in our path."

— Rabbi Barry Schwartz

Courage came first. Without it, none of these stories would exist. The courage of women and men in Ethiopia, in China and in Colorado is at the root of how I became a grandmother and learned *Mussar* from my grandchildren.

The journey took not only bravery, but also patience. When my daughter, Heidi, moved back to Colorado after graduate school, we developed the habit of mother-daughter hikes in the woods. Heidi confided that she wanted to start a family, and I encouraged her. Stopping at a sunlit spot in the forest, we meditated and prayed about her future children. After a few years, it became clear that she and her husband, Robin, couldn't have children of their own. They decided to adopt from abroad.

Heidi did not want to start the adoption process until she had saved the thousands of dollars needed to complete it. I was growing anxious to be a grandmother. After years of working fifty hours each week as communications manager for Colorado's largest school district, I had retired early and finally had the time to spend with grandchildren. I was eager to see the wonders of the world through a child's eyes without having to worry about the day-to-day burdens of parenting. I fantasized about taking my imagined grandchildren to the aquarium and the museum and teaching them about nature through walks in the woods. I pictured grandchildren as pure joy.

I watched the special relationships between my friends and their grandchildren. My mother was a grandmother at forty-four, and here I was, almost sixty, with no grandchildren in sight. *How long would we have to wait? Would it ever happen? Would I be too old to hold them, run after them, and play with them by the time — if ever — they came?*

"It's going to take years anyway. Why don't you apply now?" I urged Heidi.

Instead of a completed adoption application, she handed me a green-gray polished stone engraved with the word "patience."

Finally Heidi and Robin were ready to submit the paperwork to the adoption agency. They got the mandated background checks, took the required classes and waited. Four years passed with no word on when the Chinese adoption would come through. So Heidi and Robin decided to apply for a second child – this time from Ethiopia. More waiting ensued.

One evening as Irv and I walked across the parking lot in a nearby strip mall to get an ice cream cone, my cell phone rang. It was Heidi.

"We got a call. They have a baby girl for us in Ethiopia," she said, choking up with joy.

I wiped my eyes as we entered the ice cream shop and barely managed to utter through my tears, "We're going to be grandparents."

Thus began my family's first courageous journey, with two trips to Africa. The first trip went smoothly. Heidi and Robin visited the orphanage in Addis Ababa and met and played with Selam. They completed the paperwork and made plans for their return a month later.

But just two days before they were scheduled to leave for Ethiopia to pick up our little girl, they got a call from the adoption agency about a delay.

"There's a paperwork problem," Heidi sobbed when she told me. "We can't get Selam yet."

I couldn't move; I was cold with fear and loss for my daughter and myself. *Would they ever figure out the problem?* I lay in bed thinking of all that could go wrong: *Ethiopia would not let this child go. The embassy would not cooperate. Selam would spend the rest of her life in an orphanage, and I would never meet her.*

Heidi and Robin had held their little girl. And just when she was within arm's reach, she was snatched back. Days turned into weeks with no word. It took all the faith and courage I could muster to avoid drowning in dread.

Finally, a month later, the adoption agency called to report the paperwork snafu was resolved, and Heidi and Robin could return to Ethiopia to fetch Selam.

The morning of Friday, Feb. 4, 2011, I waited anxiously by the phone, anticipating the family's arrival back in the United States. I jumped to answer when the caller ID displayed Heidi's cell number.

"Selam is eating her first French fries," Heidi announced. They were in the DC airport, exhausted from the seventeen-hour plane ride but elated to be back, this time with toddler in tow.

The next day, Irv and I headed to Bailey, Colorado, to meet our new granddaughter. Heidi sat cross-legged in the mudroom, the toddler on her lap. Wearing a red, yellow and blue striped T-shirt and navy blue sweat pants, almost bald, with the protruding belly of a starving baby, twenty-month-old Selam greeted us with a smile, her wide brown eyes, framed in long, curled lashes, staring up at her new grandparents. We sat down next to her and after a short time, she bravely came up to me, took me by the hand and led me to her new bedroom. It was the start of my great adventure as Grandma Moo. I was in heaven.

Every day with Selam was a gift as we watched her flourish and grow. My dream of having a grandchild to take to the zoo and the park had come true. We spent Fridays together and became best buddies.

Yet our family was not complete. We were still waiting for the child from China. Six years had passed since Heidi and Robin had first filed the paperwork, and still we heard nothing.

How long was this process going to take? Would Selam grow up as an only child? My happiness was dampened by the fear that there was a child in China waiting for a family — our family — and the bureaucracy prevented our fated union.

Then one summer morning in 2012, Heidi received a second phone call from the adoption agency.

"I just got a call, Mom. They asked if we'd take a boy from China."

"Oh my God, a grandson," I exclaimed, an unexpected and delightful gift. I was filled with questions. "How old is he? What do we know about him? When do you go?"

"We know nothing yet. It was just a preliminary call," Heidi said.

Thankfully, the details came only a few days later, along with a picture of an impossibly adorable little boy with big brown eyes and a serious expression. The toddler, Dian, from rural China, was living in a foster home after being found abandoned in front of a hospital about a year earlier. The authorities had given him a name and estimated his birth date as Feb. 8, 2010.

Heidi and Robin decided they wanted to take Selam with them to China to meet her new brother, and I was invited to go along. I thought about the complications. *Did I have the ametz lev to put my life on hold and travel across the world, living for two weeks in a series of hotels with two toddlers fussing in the room next door? Did I have the patience to complete the tedious pages of paperwork, get the required inoculations and make arrangements for others to complete my volunteer obligations?* Despite the challenges, there was no way I would pass up this opportunity. I responded with an enthusiastic "yes."

Finally, after years of waiting and weeks of preparing, the day of the long journey to China arrived. Heidi, Robin and Selam picked me up before dawn to go to the airport. After a stopover in San Francisco, we headed to Hong Kong. The prolonged flight with an active toddler on a crowded aircraft made us all tired and cranky.

At long last, we deplaned and headed into the cavernous, crowded luggage hall. I grew increasingly anxious when I couldn't find my suitcase in the mounds of bags blocked by throngs of travelers elbowing their way to the front of the line. As I felt myself getting irritable, I faced a *bechirah* point. *Could I mindfully face the travel challenges with courage and patience as I remembered the long-awaited purpose of the trip*

— to fetch our grandchild? Taking a deep breath, I inched closer to the baggage carousel and soon found my luggage.

The next day, travel weary, we took a bus tour of Hong Kong. At Aberdeen Harbor, we boarded a rustic wooden boat festooned with dozens of brightly colored good luck charms. The adults admired the massive floating restaurant, with seats for 2,300 diners, but Selam was more interested in the stuffed toy rabbit hanging from the boat's steering wheel. She caressed its soft fur and held tight. She boldly looked into the eyes of the captain, asking without words if she could have it.

As we pulled back into the dock, Captain Doris unhooked the stuffed animal and handed it to Selam.

"It's been on hundreds of tours. Now it's yours." Our guide interpreted Doris' words. Selam grabbed it to her little chest and grinned.

The next morning we flew to Nanchang in southeast China and began settling into our adjoining rooms in the four-star, high-rise hotel. We waited with a mix of trepidation and anticipation for the arrival of the two-year-old newcomer to our family. Soon there was a knock on Heidi's door. I stayed hidden in my bedroom to avoid overwhelming Dian with too many strangers at once. Through the walls, I could barely hear the social workers' words of instruction, overpowered by the heart-wrenching sobs of a small child.

After about ten minutes, the crying subsided. I cracked open the door between our two rooms, and Heidi nodded that I could enter. Dian, dressed in bright orange Chinese pajamas and sporting a buzz cut, was still in Heidi's arms as the rest of the family surrounded him. Selam rubbed his back and showed him her stuffed rabbit as he peered down through his tears.

Finally, Dian mustered the courage to leave Heidi's arms and sit on the floor. He smiled for the first time as Selam chased him between the twin beds.

"Dian has been fed almost exclusively rice cereal, so be careful introducing new foods," the social workers had warned.

Yet the next morning, he eagerly eyed the plates full of food at the hotel's sumptuous breakfast buffet. There were rows of American fare, omelets, hard-boiled eggs and Danish pastries, as well as aisles filled with Chinese rice, soup and mixtures of noodles and meats.

Heidi filled Dian's plate with some bland food — hard-boiled eggs and a variety of melons. She also chose a walnut-sized Chinese fruit with a soft brown shell, but we had no idea how to eat it. We were surprised when Dian picked it up, bit into the shell to crack it open, and then expertly extracted the white fruit. He popped the fruit into his mouth, removing and presenting us with a small, deep purple pit. We daringly followed suit, savoring what we learned later was the dragon's eye fruit, similar to a lychee.

Over the next few days, Dian showed *ametz lev* as he adapted to an outgoing older sister who wanted to chase him around the room and "share" toys. And he bravely began to connect to a new family, who smelled different and spoke a strange language. Each day in Nanchang, Dian's smiles increased.

It was hard to create a new family in a hotel room. I wanted to help as much as possible, and also knew that my role as grandma was a supporting one. It was critical that Dian bonded with his new parents, and Selam needed parental attention as the now-displaced only child.

"I want to sit next to you. Put him down," Selam demanded of her mother as we took a mini-van tour of the city.

I was painfully transported back to my first day as a three-year-old big sister, watching my power as only child and first grandchild usurped when a newborn came into our lives. I had been staying with my grandmother while my mother spent four days in the hospital with the new baby. When Mom and the new baby got home, my father came to Grandma's to fetch me.

"Let's go meet your new sister," he said, taking me by the hand and walking me the few short blocks to our cramped apartment. I peered in the crib at the sleeping lump.

"Take her back," I demanded.

My father again grabbed my hand. "Come watch the Brooklyn Dodgers on TV with me," he said, leading me into the living room and away from my new rival. *He didn't take the baby with us. I'm still special to him*, I thought, reassured of my role in the family.

Remembering the fear of being replaced, I understood what Selam needed, and I silently vowed to always be there for her. For the rest of the trip, I made sure that Selam got a good chunk of my attention.

"Let's watch *Curious George* on my laptop," I said, leading her into my adjoining hotel room when she got pouty because Heidi was tending to Dian.

I held tight to her hand when we all ventured to Yuexiu Park, a massive outdoor oasis with lakes, restaurants and an amusement park. Maneuvering through the streets of Guangzhou, China's fifth-largest city, with a population of more than fifteen million, took another kind of daring.

To get to the park, we had to descend into the bowels of the subway station where we dodged hordes of hurried commuters. Emerging on the other side, we negotiated our way through groups of tourists, women practicing tai chi and bandstands filled with men playing the two-stringed fiddle and the bamboo flute. Finally we arrived at the small amusement park filled with enticing kiddy rides.

Selam, willing to try anything, dashed to the yellow, red and green airplanes while Dian, more cautious, lagged behind. Pulling him by the hand, she wordlessly convinced her new brother to board the circling planes, then the boats and the merry-go-round.

Grabbing my cell phone before I could react, Selam boldly took a picture of two soldiers in uniform sitting on a park bench sharing a smoke. I had been warned to be careful about whom we photographed in this communist nation, but Selam had no such concerns. Luckily, the soldiers pointed and laughed rather than confiscating my phone.

Every day in this foreign land provided small adventures in *ametz lev*, like wending our way through the crowded streets with two toddlers in tow to a restaurant, using sign language to get help with the menu and tasting strange delicacies, then navigating the streets in reverse to get back to our hotel.

After two weeks, we were exhausted and grateful when the time came to travel back to Colorado. On the plane ride home, Selam, the brazen social butterfly, wandered the aisle to make faces or share stories with fellow passengers. Dian spent hours quietly entertaining himself by placing little stickers on the front cover of the United Airlines magazine and then gingerly removing them to re-stick them on the back cover. Their different approaches to a long, boring plane ride foreshadowed the divergent personalities that would continue to unfold over the ensuing years.

I thought about how the adoption of my two grandchildren from exceptionally different cultures across the world offered multiple *Mussar* lessons in *ametz lev*. The first courageous act we witnessed came from Abeba, an abandoned young mother in rural Ethiopia who allowed her infant daughter to survive by relinquishing her to the local orphanage. The promise of a better life for baby Selam in a faraway place gave Abeba the courage to say goodbye, knowing she most likely would never see her child again.

The nameless, unknown parents of Dian showed yet another act of *ametz lev* and hope. They had left Dian, a skinny eighteen-month-old in diapers, deserted in front of the local hospital. No note, no explanation, just a little boy waiting alone. His parents couldn't appear; the police would most likely arrest them.

Why call that courage rather than indifferent abandonment? Looking through my *Mussar* lens, I reached a *bechirah* point. Rather than guess or criticize the reason for their decision, I would judge on the side of merit. I chose to see their choice as an act of trust and hope. By bravely leaving him at the hospital, they anticipated he would have access to a better life.

Closer to home, I admired the courage of my daughter, Heidi, and her husband, Robin. They had thoughtfully decided on foreign adoptions, waited for the right time to apply, sustained hope over many years of waiting and welcomed two children from foreign lands into their home. These acts of courage made me, at long last, a grandma, nicknamed Moo, and Irv a grandpa, nicknamed Poo.

Journal prompts
- What stories of *ametz lev* inspire you?
- How do you experience courage?
- When is courage required in your life?
- Write about a time that you acted courageously.

Mindfulness — *Zehirut*

"The only thing happening is this present moment, which is going so fast that we have almost lost it before it is even here."

— Jetsunma Tenzin Palmo

A warm, cloudless Colorado Saturday morning — all felt right in the world. I had no obligations, nowhere else I had to be, nothing else to do but enjoy this day at Heidi's home to celebrate her birthday.

We had talked about bringing pancake batter and cooking it together for brunch, but Robin, the gourmet chef, had informed us that he was whipping up a special birthday treat. The last time we had visited, it was slow-roasted duck with freshly steamed artichokes.

I was sunning in the backyard with Heidi, Irv, five-year-old Selam and four-year-old Dian while Robin created a feast that included a spinach and cheddar cheese frittata; diced, pan-fried white and sweet potatoes; and an alluring tray of blueberries, strawberries and melon.

If I can just let go of my normal behavior of constantly doing rather than being, perhaps I can find joy in the company of family and the beauty around me, I thought.

I resolved to observe every detail of my surroundings — an expansive yard with typical Colorado foothills flora; pine trees and aspens in full leaf lining the driveway, suffused in summer sunlight; a hammock hung between two blue spruces. Intermingled with the wild grasses were kids' toys — a sandbox, plastic yellow Tonka trucks, a Barbie tricycle and a pink two-wheeler.

Across the driveway, a chipped Mexican clay oven and a brick-bordered fire pit stood empty, superfluous on this warm July day. A ragtag collection of canvas, wood and metal chairs surrounded a weather-worn picnic table. Two vegetable gardens, protected from the deer by wire fencing, showed early promise, with small green leaves of kale, arugula and lettuce sprouting from the soil.

At the far end of the yard, next to the wooden storage shed, a rusty metal swing set placed next to an orange and blue plastic climbing contraption stood in stark contrast to the natural beauty of Mount Rosalie, still snowcapped, in the background.

Heidi and Irv sat down at the wooden picnic table to wait for brunch. Selam settled in the hammock.

"Will you swing with me?" Dian asked.

We walked hand-in-hand to the edge of the yard. Perching on the plastic seat, I bent my knees just enough to get my feet a few inches off the ground. Dian sat on the adjacent swing, pumping as hard as his skinny little legs allowed.

"I miss you," Dian said.

"I'm right here next to you," I replied, confused. In my reality, I was giving him just what he wanted: some special time with grandma.

But wait. Indeed I was sitting right next to Dian. My attention, however, was elsewhere. I was straining to eavesdrop on the conversation between my husband and daughter, fifty yards away. They were talking about the challenges of child-rearing. Maybe I could offer my expert advice from across the yard.

Physically, I was "right here" next to my grandson, but mentally, not so much. Dian got it before I did. I was not fully present, and Dian knew it. My actions did not reflect my goal of truly being with him.

During my career as communications manager, I was often required to simultaneously respond to competing demands, especially during a crisis. When the World Trade Center tragedy occurred on Sept. 11, 2001, I worked frantically to produce up-to-date information for our 120 schools. The head of our school counseling department sat next to me in my office while I talked on the phone and simultaneously typed a list of crisis counseling tips to send to the schools.

"Boy, can you multi-task!" the counselor exclaimed. I grinned, proud to accept the compliment.

But today, Dian's reception to my divided attention was the reverse. *How could I bring my Mussar study to the situation?* I wondered.

"The practice of mindfulness has as its intention to continue to observe what is arising from moment to moment in one's experience," says Rabbi Sheila Peltz Weinberg.

At this moment with Dian, my intention was to give him my full attention. Yet my habit of trying to do more than one thing at a time, and not wanting to miss any adult conversation, was getting in the way.

I was faced with a *bechirah* point. What would I choose — adult conversation or attending to my grandson?

The answer was obvious. I stopped trying to eavesdrop, turned to face Dian, and began a conversation.

"What do you want to talk about?" I asked.

"Tell me a story about dinosaurs."

"Once upon a time there was a stegosaurus," I began.

A few weeks later, I had another opportunity for a *bechirah* point in being present for Dian. Selam and Dian had begun asking if they could take turns having some "alone time" with me. So one Saturday morning, Heidi dropped Dian off and left with Selam to run errands.

What an opportunity! I hadn't realized until that moment how I had deprived Kevin's and Heidi's two grandmothers of a great gift. Irv and I had moved across the country before our kids were born, and our mothers never had the good fortune of a drop-in visit with grandchildren. Only when they made an annual, weeklong trek to Colorado did the grandmas have the chance to bond with our children.

And I had missed out too. There were no nearby loving babysitters to share the joys and stresses of child rearing. As a working mother of young children, I often needed to apply my multi-tasking skills at home as well as in the office. I always had household chores looming –

laundry, dishes, vacuuming. I half listened to Heidi's and Kevin's stories about what happened on the school bus as I cooked spaghetti pie in the kitchen. I folded towels while we watched cartoons. I left them to their homework as I ironed my skirt and blouse for the next day.

Now, as a grandmother, I had the gifts of time and proximity to grandkids. I could sit and play on the floor during a drop-in visit and ignore household duties and unreturned emails. After all, the kids would go home in a few hours and the chores could wait. And yet, in this fast-paced world where multi-tasking is not only expected but also rewarded, it was sometimes hard to remember to be fully present, to resist the temptation of doing more than one thing at a time.

Dian took me by the hand and brought me into the bedroom.

"What do you want to do?" I asked.

He looked around at his toys — Hot Wheels cars, a jungle puzzle, a Candyland game — and opened up the plastic container with a set of wooden IKEA trains and tracks. He began attaching the tracks, twisting and turning the pieces until they fit together. Then he took the black engine, green coal car and red caboose from the container, trying to get the magnets to match up. Frustrated, he handed me two cars that he couldn't make stick together.

"You have to turn them around, so the magnets attract each other." *Magnets have to face each other in the right direction to create connection; humans connect through zehirut,* I reflected.

Adding a few more cars, he raced the train around the wooden track. I picked up the remaining cars and created my own train chain, and we started in opposite directions around the winding track, colliding head-on with giggles as our trains derailed.

When he had had his fill of crashing trains, Dian asked if I would read him a book. He chose *I Think I Can* about the little engine that struggled up the hill with help from his friends and a positive attitude. I remembered how Irv's mother had loved to read that book to my kids when she visited from Florida, and I was delighted that Dian favored the story too.

As we cuddled on the couch, I read about the train's struggle to get up a steep hill. The harsh, demanding ringing of the telephone interrupted. A *bechirah* point: answer the phone or stay with Dian. Against my better judgment, I dashed into the kitchen and picked up the phone. It was my sister, Ellen, and we immediately engaged in an emotional conversation about Mom's failing health.

Dian remained on the couch, his body still as he stared at me for a few minutes. Then he jumped up and began pacing across the room.

It brought back a childhood memory of sitting in our tiny apartment kitchen at the small, speckled gray Formica table, my legs dangling high above the floor, with a bowl of steaming macaroni and cheese in front of me.

The phone rang, and my mother said, "Wait for the food to cool before you eat it" as she picked up the receiver.

"Hi Minna. How are you feeling?" my mom asked.

She turned to the wall, her concentration focused on Aunt Minna's story rather than on me.

After several minutes, wanting to regain her attention, I spooned a forkful of hot, curly pasta into my mouth and started crying when the heat burned my tongue.

"I told you to wait," she sighed, exasperated as she ended the call.

Now Dian was getting impatient from the same type of interruption. After five minutes, he came up next to me and said with a pout, "You're wasting our alone time."

Chagrined, I said a quick goodbye to Ellen, promised to call back later, hung up and returned my full attention to Dian. I sat back down on the couch, my arm around Dian as I read. We grinned with satisfaction as I retold the story of how the little engine finally made it over the mountain, through intention and connecting with friends, to deliver his toys, a lesson in optimism and persistence.

And what could I learn from the effort of the little engine whose singular focus helped get him over the mountain? I wondered. Perhaps after a career of accolades for multi-tasking at work, I could learn the value of choosing one task at a time. Dian's request for my full attention was a persuasive reason to embrace the present moment. He needed and deserved it. And so did I.

Journal prompts
- What techniques do you use to stay "present?"
- What are your barriers to *zehirut*?
- Think about a time when mindfulness helped create a choice point you didn't see before.

Patience — *Savlanut*

"The essence of patience is to live in the present. We are impatient because we want to be in the future faster than reality will take us there."

— Rabbi Zelig Pliskin

Please can we have quarters for the toy machine," six-year-old Selam begged as we headed toward the exit of Big Time, the indoor trampoline park. The kids had spent an hour jumping on long, bright blue floor mats and careening down inflatable slides, yet they still had plenty of energy to expend.

"Look at those cute stuffies; I want the frog," Selam said.

"It's a waste of money," I responded. "Most of the time, you don't get a prize, and even if you do, it's worth less than the amount you put in the machine. Let's go to the Dollar Tree. You can each get three items there."

"Yay, the dollar store!" the kids shouted in unison. Holding tight to my hands, the kids pulled me across the parking lot to the shop brimming with imported treasures.

"Come on, Poo." Selam looked back at her trailing grandpa, who had lost his left leg from illness in the 1980s. His prosthesis was aching from standing at Big Time, but he gamely followed along.

Irv found a shopping cart to lean on while I sprinted to keep up with the kids, eager to get the most for their three bucks, to the toy aisle. It was lined with rows of cheaply made toys from China: glow-in-the-dark hula hoops, bubbles in pink plastic bottles shaped like ice cream cones, and anorexic Barbie doll knockoffs in stiletto heels.

Dian picked up a metallic red, plastic-wrapped Hot Wheels sedan. "I definitely want this," he proclaimed, walking farther down the aisle with the toy held tightly in his fist. He halted a few feet later to inspect the section where factory-molded rows of identical olive green soldiers hung in plastic bags from crammed hooks.

"I changed my mind, Moo," he said, handing me the car as he picked up a four-inch soldier with a white paper parachute. Continuing his saunter down the row of toys, he spotted a big blue rubber ball.

"I want this one." Stretching his arms around the ball, his eyes peering over the top, he walked to the end of the toy section and reversed direction. He returned the soldier to its hook then considered and rejected spinning tops and water balloons. He halted at the Hot Wheels display where his shopping adventure had begun. Crouching on the floor, he took all the cars, trucks, buses and motorcycles off their hooks to get a closer look until the jumble of vehicles on the well-worn industrial carpet resembled a multi-car pileup on an icy freeway.

"I already have this one," he said as he created a discard pile of miniature blue Ford pickups and green vans.

After several minutes of solemn contemplation, he handed me a flaming orange convertible and a yellow Chevy sedan, vintage 1955. "This is what I want to buy."

Meanwhile Selam, empty-handed, wandered up and down the aisle, stopping every few seconds to consider a toy.

"What's this?" She handed me a decorative pink box.

"A paper doll set."

She frowned and returned it to the shelf.

"Will you buy these bubbles as a special present for us so we can buy three other things?" she negotiated.

"If you want the bubbles, they count toward your three items." Resolving to keep my word, I replied firmly. It wasn't the dollar; it was the deal I had to protect. I wanted to teach them the value of money.

After Selam had spent fifteen minutes of picking up, only to reject, Silly Putty, an orange Whoopee cushion and a packet of neon green glow-in-the-dark bracelets, I had had enough. Irv was waiting near the entrance, still leaning on the cart for support. My feet were aching and my patience thinning.

Where, after all, had I learned patience? I was transported back to the dusty, disorganized neighborhood sporting goods store of my youth. There my father had paced back and forth as I looked through the stack of tennis rackets. I picked up each one, feeling the weight in my hand as my coach had advised. I was fourteen and taking tennis lessons after school.

"What are you, a tennis pro? Pick one already," my father snarled, his anger bubbling to the surface. I hastily grabbed the racket with the red handle, my favorite color, and handed it to my father. I trailed behind as he rushed brusquely toward the cash register.

In my family, being quick was not only valued but required to avoid Dad's wrath. I had learned to waste no time — in my choices at the store, in bringing him a glass of milk while he was watching television, when getting into the car to visit relatives. Keeping him waiting might mean a shout or worse yet, a push or a slap.

The result of growing up a in a fast-paced house in high-speed New York, where everyone dashed instead of walked, was that I was always in a rush, impatient with myself and others. I finished other people's sentences. I tapped my foot while waiting in line at the grocery store. I cursed under my breath when I hit a traffic jam on the interstate.

When I started studying *Mussar* in *Everyday Holiness* and perused the *middot*, the first one that struck me was *savlanut*.

Now that's one that I can put on the top of my list, I thought.

And where could I find better teachers than the grandkids? I remembered one of the first Fridays that Selam had spent at our house.

"Let's put on your shoes. It's time to go home," I told Selam after a day of play. She jumped on our bed and wiggled around as she giggled at my attempts to grab hold of her.

"It's time to go, *now*."

The louder my voice, the more she resisted.

"You need to help me, Selam," I shouted as I captured her in my arms and attempted to put on her shoes as she kicked her feet.

Finally I figured out that the more I hurried her, the longer it would take. As soon as I engaged in a battle of the wills, I had already lost. Raising my voice not only didn't work, I also felt worse about the interaction because I reacted in anger rather than love.

To practice *savlanut*, I had to become more aware of what triggered my impatience and make the choice to stop and think before I reacted. I worked on "opening the space between the match and the fuse," as Alan Morinis' *Mussar* teacher, Rabbi Perr, had advised him. I acknowledged Selam's feelings while setting limits.

"I know you're having fun playing the *Frozen* card game. We can play one more round, and then it's time to get ready to go home," I said, alerting her that it was almost time to leave.

I tried the same strategy at the Dollar Tree.

"There are so many toys, so it's hard to choose, isn't it? But if we stay much longer, you won't have time to play at my house. You have two more minutes, and then we need to go to the front to pay." My voice calm, I made the choice to check my growing impatience.

Selam quickly grabbed the next thing she saw, a king-size faux diamond ring, off the shelf and put it in our cart next to her packages of balloons and *Frozen* stickers. Dian rushed back down the aisle to return the rubber ball to its rightful place and chose a neon green Hot Wheels car to add to the other two.

As we headed to the cashier, Selam abruptly made a U-turn, testing my patience once again as she bought another minute in the toy aisle.

"Wait," she said and hurriedly exchanged the ring for a kite adorned with Disney princesses. I took a deep breath and remembered it was a lesson in money for them and patience for me.

Only one cash register was open, and the cashier was helping an elderly woman with a basket filled with outdoor paraphernalia. Lifting each item from the cart with great care and placing them gingerly on the conveyor belt, the customer extracted seat cushions, a wrought iron bird cage and plastic orange flower pots.

Eager to get to the car and play with her treasures, Selam boomed, "She has too much stuff. Why isn't there another line?"

"Maybe no one else is working," I whispered. "We can practice our patience." I suppressed a smirk at the irony of my remark.

Just then, a second cashier arrived and offered to ring up our purchases. The kids eagerly raced to the new line, the lesson in *savlanut* replaced by immediate gratification as the cashier bagged the toys. The six dollars, plus tax, paid, the kids rushed across the parking lot and into the car, ripping into the plastic packaging to free and admire their purchases.

With satisfied smiles, they settled into their car seats and began playing with their toys. I, too, had a satisfied smile. I had reached a *bechirah* point, and rather than choosing my habitual reaction of impatience and harsh words, I had put space between the match and the fuse. By reacting with calm understanding yet setting reasonable limits, I was able to come from a place of love and strength.

Journal prompts
- What makes you impatient?
- How can you put more space between the match and the fuse?
- When is impatience justified?

Curiosity — *Hitlamdut*

"To curiosity we can credit the survival and expansion of our species, our sciences, and our faith. It holds the key to unlocking wonderment, to transforming the 'same-old, same-old syndrome' to something new and bold."

— Rabbi Jamie Arnold

Selam rushed into the zero-depth pool and began to splash through the jets of water as she yelped with delight. "The fountains are so high today. How come they are bigger than last time? How do they make them go up so far?" she asked with *hitlamdut*.

"There's a control room in the back. Maybe that's how they do it," I answered as she pulled me into the water.

"Come on, Moo!" she urged, a bit impatient as I tentatively entered the cool water, testing the temperature with my big toe. I adjusted my goggles, pulled on my blue bathing cap and navigated around the spouting fountains.

"Watch this," seven-year-old Selam commanded as she submerged and twisted her body round and round. Then she dashed into the lazy river, the meandering water ride with a gentle current.

"Bet you can't catch me."

Adjusting her Nemo goggles and pulling up the straps of her black-and-white striped bathing suit adorned with pink and purple flowers, she dove under the water and disappeared, curious to see if she could evade my grasp. I dutifully pursued, reaching for her long brown legs as she rounded the corner and escaped my touch. She surfaced just long enough to glance back at me and giggle.

As Selam turned the corner of the river, she was joined by a little girl with long blonde curls, dressed in a faded blue Disney princess bathing suit. Suddenly I was extraneous. Selam had found a friend.

"I'm cold," Dian complained a short while later, his knee-high wet suit offering scarce protection for his skinny body. His lips matched the purple of his garment, and his scrawny legs shook as he pleaded, "Moo, come with me to the hot tub."

We left the cool pool to submerge in the warm, bubbly water. I immediately sought out a jet to soothe my aching back while Dian walked along the perimeter of the tub, moving his hands across the water, his *hitlamdut* aroused by the ever-replenishing bubbles. His fingers moved along the hot tub wall, probing to find the water source. When he discovered a jet, he attempted to stop the flow with his hands while his lean body recovered from the chill.

"I'm ready to leave. I'm hungry," Selam said after an hour, her fingers wrinkled and her friend gone.

Childhood curiosity abounded yet again in what appeared to me as the dull, clammy family locker room. To my grandkids, the cramped changing room was filled with the promise of adventure as they took turns adjusting the shower dial to turn the spray from warm to cold and back. Selam shoved her head under the noisy hair dryer and then played with drying her arms under the blowing hot air. Dian turned off the lights, curious to see how dark the windowless room would get. Finally, done with experimenting, the kids got dressed and ready for a picnic.

Fetching the dog from the car, we headed to the small pond behind the recreation center for a picnic lunch. It was an unseasonably warm November day with a cloudless sky, and we savored the sunshine on our backs as we sat on the wooden plank dock. Selam peered over the edge into the water.

"Look down there! What's that?"

We gazed into the clear, shallow water just inches in front of us and saw a faded red crustacean, clearly long deceased.

"Is it dead or resting?" Dian asked.

"It's dead. Looks like a crayfish, but I never saw one before in a Colorado pond."

"I want to get it out, Moo. Help me find a stick," Selam insisted, grabbing me by the hand and leading me along the water's edge.

I hesitated. Did we really want to fish out that disgusting dead body with its missing claws?

I thought back to my two children's youth. If they had wanted to extract a dead animal from a stagnant pond, I would have worried about germs, dirt and a plunge into the water. I would not have encouraged science. My immediate response would have been, "Leave it alone. It's dirty, dead. Who knows what killed it? Just eat your lunch. We can look at it from here."

Though I had lived in these foothills for more than forty years, I was not naturally at home in nature. Riding beneath the concrete jungle of New York City and finding the right subway stop? No problem. Digging around in a swampy pond to pull out a dead animal? Not so much. I was not comfortable in the "wild," and I hadn't encouraged Heidi and Kevin to be comfortable there either. Yes, I took them on regular hikes on the vacant land down the road from our home, and they had named each mountain that we viewed from the top of the hill. But at other times, my discomfort was clear.

"Get that out of my house!" I trembled when I came home from work one evening to find Irv and our two toddlers playing with a plump, neon green tomato worm perched on a leaf on our glass living room table, one of my favorite pieces of furniture.

"No, we're not keeping that dirty thing. It's going back into the woods." I recoiled when the kids asked to keep a mouse as a pet after we had caught it in a live trap.

But *Mussar* and age had changed me. As a grandmother, I didn't want to dampen Selam's *hitlamdut* because I was worried she might end up dirty and damp, or at worst, soaking wet from a fall into the pond. I wanted to reward her inquisitiveness, her enthusiasm, her eagerness to "do science" in the real world. Selam had told me she didn't like science in school; the fill-in-the-blank worksheets were boring.

Now at a pond she could experience science in the outdoors, maybe learning to love it.

What's the worst that could happen? A wet kid?

I agreed to take part in the great experiment as I tried to match her curiosity rather than express my worry.

"Let's try this stick with the hot dog on top," Selam said, leaning into the water to grab a cattail and extend it toward the crayfish.

"It's too short and it's too bendy. We have to find a longer one. Come on, Moo."

Selam scampered up the hillside. I followed cautiously as I crunched the dead brown grass and fallen leaves of wintering aspens. I searched for the right tool. At the top of the hill, I saw some stiff beige stalks, a souvenir of summer, standing tall, still deep in the ground.

"These might work. Step hard on the base and try to break it off."

Selam put her sneakered toe on the edge of the bent stalk and jumped. Crack. She pulled the prize from its roots and smiled.

Running down the hill, branch in hand, Selam stopped at the edge of the dock. Patiently, she poked at the dead crustacean. She stretched her long slim body over the water, but the prize remained just out of reach. She persisted, slowly coaxing the crayfish closer to shore until she finally captured it on the edge of her stick and placed it carefully on the dock. She repeated the task with a second crayfish that she had spotted on the other side of the pier.

As we sat on the shore admiring and studying her catch, a woman walked briskly by on the path above, clearly out for exercise. Unlike us, basking in the sunshine in our T-shirts, she was bundled in a brown jacket with hood as protection from the breeze. Engaged with the grandkids, I didn't recognize her.

"Hi Marilyn," she called, continuing to stride down the trail.

"Oh, hi Susan," I responded.

She barely slowed for the pleasantries, bent on keeping up her speed and her heart rate. But her intentions were no match for Selam's unbridled enthusiasm.

"Come see what we found," Selam shouted, and my friend, a

grandmother herself, paused and climbed down the steep dirt hill to the small wooden dock. Susan stopped halfway down to pet the dog.

"Come on, come see this," Selam persisted.

Carefully laid out on the planks on their backs were the two dead, almost intact crayfish. "Look at their claws. This one is missing a couple." Selam pointed, captivated by her capture.

"Wow, there are crayfish in the pond? I had no idea," Susan said, suitably impressed.

"Yes, and there are other fish too," Selam exclaimed. "I saw three of them swimming. They're alive."

"There are only two. That was a shadow," Dian replied.

Selam peered into the water. "Look, there are three of them. I can see them now. I told you." Selam jumped up and down. "Can we please feed them?"

Susan bade us farewell and continued her walk while we remained on the dock, looking for something suitable in the green insulated lunch box to feed the three trout.

Dian fished some goldfish crackers from a plastic bag and threw a couple into the lake.

A red-striped fish jumped out of the water, making a pass at the crackers. But we were too close for its comfort.

"Throw one a little farther out," I said.

Dian stood up, pulled back his skinny arm, and pitched the cracker over the dock.

The trout jumped again, this time capturing the food on the fly to the sound of the kids' enthralled yelps.

"Another one, another one," Selam shouted. "Can I throw one in?"

Dian handed her a goldfish cracker; she threw; the trout responded. Ten minutes of entertainment ensued until we ran out of "fish food."

As the fish swam off, we decided to leave the pond. On the way up the hill to the car, we talked about what we had learned about crayfish and trout.

"I didn't know there were trout in the pond," I said.

"And they like goldfish crackers," Dian remarked.

"And the crayfish have eight little claws; some fall off when they die," Selam added.

I had allowed the kids to experiment, and the wonders of nature had come alive for all of us. As Rabbi Nancy Fuchs-Kreimer says, "Kids see the universe in a grain of sand more easily than we do. They are a lot closer to the ground, and they spend more time getting their hands dirty."

"The leaves falling off the trees are not dead, they are just sleeping," Dian assured me one fall day as I drove him home from preschool, my tires crunching on gold and red leaves through an aspen grove.

"Sleeping?"

"The leaves will wake up next spring when it's warm again."

Standing in the backyard and looking up in the sky, Selam proclaimed to me, "I'm going to take a magic carpet ride to the clouds and eat them."

"What do you think they'll taste like?"

"Like Chanukah and Christmas and Halloween and lollipops and candy canes."

Through a *Mussar* lens and the play of energetic grandchildren, I was transformed from the squeamish city girl to the curious grandma. I experienced firsthand what Rabbi Sam Feinsmith wrote, "To get a sense of beginner's mind, observe young children at play — how they are in the moment, completely open to the flow of experience just as it is. Without preconceived notions about how things should be, children are able to relate to the most ordinary experiences with an innate sense of curiosity, wonder, and radical amazement."

Lessons in lifecycles and imagination, the ordinary transformed to extraordinary and all God's handiwork became exciting and new, thanks to my favorite young teachers.

Journal prompts
- When did you last look at the world through the eyes of a child?
- How can you foster "a beginner's mind"?
- How might a curious approach to a difficult experience change your experience?

Generosity — *Nedivut*

"If you see a person giving liberally, it means his wealth will grow; if you see one who shuns charity, it means his wealth will dwindle."
— Midrash Mishle on Book of Proverbs

Though I was a frequent visitor to Mrs. O's kindergarten room, it took me a few seconds to adjust to the cacophony of sights and sounds that confronted me as I entered. A casino in Las Vegas could not provide more sensory stimulation. It was a sunny May afternoon near the end of a school day at the end of the school year. The twenty-five animated kindergartners had just celebrated Madeline's birthday with chocolate mini-brownies purchased at Costco.

I did not immediately spot five-year-old Dian among the kindergartners chatting and squirming in bright blue kiddy chairs clustered around red, green and blue tables. Arranged in parallel and perpendicular patterns, the tables were surrounded by a sea of shelves filled with water bottles and lunchboxes, hooks heavy with princess and superhero jackets, and walls crammed with words and drawings.

A squat kelly green table, work station for my grandson and five others, closely abutted a fire-engine red table. Short, dark-haired Dian sat almost back-to-back with tall, blonde Ethan who was at the red table. If both boys got up at the same time, a collision of chairs was almost certain. Yet the configuration seemed to work under Mrs. O's careful tutelage, and instead of head butting, Dian and Ethan became good friends.

While my first impression was chaos, a closer look proved that every inch of wall space provided a teaching opportunity — days of the week and months of the year, and sight words for the week — up, this, here, there.

In the back of the room, a wooden rocking chair faced a patchwork carpet where the children gathered, sitting "crisscross applesauce" (cross-legged) with their "hands in their basket" (laps) when Mrs. O read aloud or gave instructions on a math concept.

I was struck by the blue-lined chart paper with kid-developed classroom norms that hung crookedly at one end of the chalkboard. Some of the norms focused on safety — *don't throw things, use your voice instead of your hands* — while others stressed kindness — *take turns, share with your neighbors.*

Words about sharing brought me back to my own childhood. When my siblings and I were arguing over the last cookie, my mother repeated the story about fighting with her sister over the only glass of fresh-squeezed orange juice, resulting in its landing on the floor, smashing into pieces and staining the linoleum orange. "Being selfish means you all lose," she had warned us.

As a parent and grandparent, I expected to mediate selfishness in children, yet I also experienced examples of generosity and sharing. A few weeks before, when we were making cookies, Selam and Dian both wanted to stir the dough.

"You do it, Selam," Dian said after a few moments of disagreement.

"Why did you let her stir when you wanted to?" I asked.

"Because I want my sister to be happy."

The kindergartners were cleaning up the dessert crumbs when, adding to the excitement, Mrs. O announced she was going to give away old costumes from the supply closet.

"You can choose one item from each of the bins," she said, dragging two large, transparent plastic containers to the front of the classroom. One bin was filled with cowboy hats, camouflage Army caps and red feather boas. The other held gossamer wings of translucent gold, red and blue with Velcro straps.

The teacher picked up a tin can filled with tongue depressors, each with a student's name in black marker, to randomly select students to make their choices from the two bins. I admired how she modeled fairness. Yet as grandma, I silently prayed that Dian's name would be one of the first ones called, worried that there might be no "good stuff" left by the time Mrs. O pulled his stick from the blue can.

So I sat on my knees, next to Dian's pint-sized chair, leaning close. I could feel his excitement and eagerness to get a special cap. "Olivia," the teacher called, and a freckled girl with shoulder-length blonde hair jumped out of the seat next to Dian's, wending her way among eager classmates to the two bins. She peered inside and picked up red fairy wings, then gold ones, before finally settling on a pair of pastel blue. Without hesitation, she pulled a red boa from the second bin.

"Troy," the teacher read as she pulled a second stick from the bucket. Bounding to the front of the room, button-nosed Troy selected a green, white and beige camouflage cap from the first container and bee's wings from the second.

Mrs. O continued calling students to the front of the room. Waiting patiently, Dian told me, "I don't want any wings. I just want a cap." Finally Mrs. O announced his name. He walked up to the wing basket, peered in, and despite what he had said, selected big red ones decorated with black hearts. The hat selection was an easy choice — an Army camouflage baseball cap.

Dian walked proudly back to his seat, treasures in hand.

"I got the wings for my sister." He placed the hat on his head and turned to his buddy. "I got the same one as you, Troy."

Mrs. O reminded them to put their treasures in their backpacks, and Dian quickly obeyed, stuffing the red wings between his lunch box and the stack of drawings he had created. The hat was placed gently on top before he zipped up his well-worn Thomas the Train backpack.

I helped Ellie wedge pink fairy wings into her Princess Elsa pack and zipped it most of the way as the teacher continued to call names. With a classroom full of kids making difficult choices, it was taking a while to get through them all.

"Ethan," Mrs. O shouted over the din of the students excitedly cramming their hats and wings into already stuffed backpacks, or jumping up and down awaiting their turn.

"Finally," Ethan sighed as he leapt out of his chair and approached the bins. He immediately chose a pair of blue wings from the first bin, but only bright red feather boas were left in the second. He took one reluctantly, and tears rolled down his face as he plopped into his seat.

"What's wrong, Ethan?" Dian asked.

"I wanted an Army hat," he replied between gasps.

Without missing a beat, Dian pulled the cap out of his backpack and handed it to Ethan, exchanging it for the red boa. Ethan clutched the cap in his hand, the tears evaporating into a smile.

"This is for you, Moo," Dian said, stuffing the boa into his backpack. "I'll give it to you when we get home."

Generosity, kindness and compassion were all rolled into one simple act by a five-year-old. Only Dian's table mates and I witnessed the act. No one spoke.

A few days later, I visited school during recess. The two-level playground featured a concrete pad with basketball hoops and some play equipment on the upper deck while the lower play area was set in the natural environment, surrounded by pine trees. Dian and Ethan ran amidst the tall pines as Marc and Jeffrey chased them. Ethan spotted a dead branch of a spruce tree lying on the ground. He stopped, picked up the three-foot branch and began to study it. Then he plucked a couple of pine needles, still green, and handed them to me.

"For you."

"Thank you," I said, grasping the treasure in my fingers. I opened the zipper of my purse and gently placed the gift inside.

Later that afternoon, Olivia, the blonde sitting next to Dian, handed me the picture she had been creating. "You can have this one," she said, pushing an abstract of crayon-drawn, misshapen circles across the table toward me. It was another gift that I gratefully, yet quizzically, accepted.

Not until later did it strike me that the two children who had witnessed Dian's acts of spontaneous *nedivut* earlier in the week had reciprocated with a gift to his grandma. Was it a coincidence, a conscious act of reciprocity or an unconscious response to modeling?

— ❤ —

A few weeks later, walking Togo, our old black Lab, along the dirt roads of our neighborhood, I spotted a little boy with long blonde curls toddling into the quiet street. His father followed closely enough to keep the boy safe and far enough to allow some freedom. They had come up the driveway from the stucco home, painted the color of chocolate mousse, which I had always admired.

The boy, wearing blue jeans, a plaid shirt and red sneakers, wobbled toward me on learner's legs. I stopped short and grasped the leash tightly about a foot from Togo's body. Though an old man in years, Togo often still acted like a puppy. If we had been at home, Togo would have greeted the visitor by jumping up to lick his face or wagging his tail so hard that the barely balanced toddler would have dropped to the ground. But today Togo stood perfectly still.

The boy approached, patted Togo on the back and explored the old dog's nose and gray muzzle with pudgy fingers. Chatting with the dad, I watched the child stoop to the ground and pick up a black pebble. He shuffled over to me, treasure extended. I opened my hand, and he placed the small rock in it.

"Thank you for the present," I said, stooping down to see him eye-to-eye. He smiled and stood next to his dad as we continued talking for a few minutes. It was the third gift from a child in as many weeks.

It wasn't the first time I had experienced an unexpected act of *nedivut* from a child. Several years before we were on a South Pacific cruise, and the ship docked on the island of Bora Bora. We decided to escape the crowds by renting a car for the day and exploring the island on our own. Driving down a country road, we stopped to admire a tall banana tree with almost ripe fruit surrounded by cherry red hibiscus trees. I was so engaged in photographing the foliage that I didn't notice the barefoot teenager crossing the street until she was right there.

I jumped as she came up behind me.

Is she going to ask for money?

I remembered being surrounded by a dozen street children in Mexico, reaching up to me and pleading to sell me "goma." I recalled men with dirty, unkempt hair dressed in layers of soiled clothing, loitering inside the Manhattan subway stations, coming close enough I could smell alcohol on their breath as they begged for spare change. These awkward incidents always created an uncomfortable *bechirah* point. Should I act with *nedivut* or fearful withdrawal?

With a wary smile, I backed away as the young Bora Boran grew closer. Then she plucked a hibiscus flower from the tree and gently placed it behind my ear.

"Thank you," I said in surprise, chagrined by my unfounded suspicions. She smiled shyly, her long, silky black hair waving in the wind as she crossed the street without a word, disappearing into the lush foliage around her home as quickly as she had appeared.

What did these unbidden, spontaneous acts of children's generosity come to teach me? Observing these acts of kindness through a *Mussar* lens made me stop and think about the true nature of *nedivut*. In *Everyday Holiness*, Alan Morinis points out that there are two kinds of generosity in Jewish tradition — obligatory giving, from a sense of duty, and giving that comes from the heart "without even the flicker of thought."

I had learned to practice obligatory giving — making charitable contributions to nonprofits, bringing canned goods to food drives and buying raffle tickets at fundraisers. The children in my life had demonstrated the second kind of *nedivut*, giving from the heart. Witnessing these unplanned acts of kindness, I learned the value of practicing the soul trait of generosity with greater spontaneity. Giving from the heart required being mindful, seeing the needs of others and responding lovingly to them.

These experiences also reminded me that life is full of *bechirah* points. I can judge on the side of merit and expect the best from every interaction, or I can assume the worst. I can be wary of an approaching stranger or open myself to her gifts. When my heart and mind are open, I can welcome spontaneous acts of generosity with joy and gratitude.

Journal prompts
- When is the last time you received a spontaneous act of generosity? How did it feel?
- When have you performed an act of generosity from the heart? How did it feel?
- How has a child taught you about *nedivut*?
- When might you try judging on the side of merit?

Trust — *Bitachon*

"The goal of Trust is to let go of worry and control, to learn that whatever happens, you will be able to deal with it."

— Greg Marcus

Just a few months after she arrived from Ethiopia, not yet two years old, Selam came with a group of our friends to a Mexican restaurant in nearby Golden. Coors employees and School of Mines students filled the booths and tables crammed together against walls decorated with posters of bullfighters and Flamenco dancers.

The hostess in her red, yellow and green flare skirt led our group to the back room as we wended our way through an obstacle course of diners and waitresses holding trays of sizzling fajitas and steamy tortilla soup. I gripped Selam's hand as she toddled down the narrow passageway between booths and tables.

Passing a booth with two young women, she spotted a woven straw basket of tortilla chips near the edge of the table. Before I could react, Selam reached up and grabbed a crunchy chip, then crammed it into her mouth. The two diners laughed in surprise as I apologized and lifted Selam in my arms before she snatched more.

We sat down at the long, wooden rectangular table, large enough to hold our group of a dozen retired educators who met monthly for lunch and fellowship. We settled in and the waitress arrived with chips, still warm and crisp from the oven. Selam reached for the basket and began grabbing with both hands. Her cheeks puffed like a chipmunk's as she stuffed morsels into her mouth.

"Our food will be here soon. Let's not fill up on chips." Distracting her with a toy, I handed the basket to a friend who moved it to the other side of the table.

When the waitress brought my enchilada platter, I made a plate for Selam. She gobbled the food, and her eager eyes wandered across the table, looking for more from my friends — quesadillas, tamales, rice.

She walked around the table, accepting anything anyone would share. She did not discriminate between chips and beans, lettuce or fish. Though she had not yet acquired any English words, her intentions were clear. Selam pointed, grabbed or looked sweetly into the eyes of our friends and got whatever she wanted. She even charmed the waitress, who carried her into the kitchen, bringing her back with a warm sopapilla in hand. We left the restaurant with a happy little girl, tummy filled.

Later that summer, my sister, Ellen, came to visit and meet Selam. Robin prepared one of his famous antipasto dishes, a tray brimming with artichoke hearts, green and black olives, roasted red peppers, white and yellow cheese, and cherry tomatoes drizzled with home-made, lemon-laced dressing. We passed the tray around the picnic table, savoring the food, the conversation and the antics of our new grandchild. Again, Selam finished every last bite on her plate, from the cheese to the veggies, and then climbed on the lap of each guest to beg for more.

"Wow, what an appetite," Ellen remarked. "I can't believe how much she can eat."

My sister had been one of those picky childhood eaters. Frustrated and worried because Ellen would turn up her nose at any food she cooked, my mother had asked our family physician for advice. He suggested that if Ellen didn't finish her oatmeal at breakfast, my mother refrigerate it and serve it again at lunch; it was a cruel punishment that didn't work. After all, even the best eater would likely refuse cold, lumpy oatmeal. Finally, our neighbor Charlotte came to the rescue. She invited Ellen to lunch, and Ellen fell in love with Charlotte's tuna salad, which became my sister's mainstay.

My son, Kevin, had also been a fussy eater. His vegetable of choice was French fries; if a food was green, he'd abandon it on his plate. And he refused to try anything new. One day, a group of friends brought over pizza. They tried to bribe Kevin with a quarter, then upped the ante to fifty cents (a significant bribe for a preschooler in the 1970s) if Kevin would just try a mushroom-laden slice of pizza.

"No way." Kevin had turned away and grabbed a slice untainted with fungi.

And here was Selam, stuffing every morsel into her mouth. I attributed her appetite to the fact that she came to our family from Ethiopia as an eighteen-month-old with the swollen belly of a malnourished child. Abeba, her biological mother, had made the heart-breaking decision to relinquish Selam because both of them were starving to death. When Heidi and Robin adopted her, they were given a list of foods that Selam had been fed at the orphanage: injera, the spongy sourdough bread of Ethiopia, with lentils, beans and small bits of meat. But all Heidi and Robin had seen her eat was barley gruel, and she had a severe case of giardiasis.

Of course, she'll eat everything in sight, I thought, *she can't get enough in her belly to make up for her first eighteen months. She's hungry!*

Yet looking through my *Mussar* lens, I saw Selam's voracious appetite from a different perspective. *Mussar* teachers often use the story of the "manna test" to teach about *bitachon*.

After the Israelites crossed the Sea of Reeds on their escape from slavery in Egypt, God fostered their capacity for trust by providing manna, but only enough for that day. If the newly freed slaves attempted to stockpile the food, it rotted. By imparting just enough, God was building — and testing — *bitachon* among the Israelites. Soon they learned that God would provide; they did not need to hoard.

Selam was teaching us a modern-day version of the same lesson. When she first saw the plentiful food, she couldn't stop herself from eating everything she could get her hands on — just like the Israelites in the desert. She went far beyond fulfilling her hunger; she was eating because she didn't know if there would be food the next time she was hungry. After suffering starvation early in life, how could she be sure that this abundance would continue?

In the first few months she was in our family, Selam woke up in the middle of the night crying for food, not necessarily because she was hungry, but because she needed to make sure it was still there. She demanded food after waking up from a nap. She tried to open the refrigerator and help herself at all times of day, even right after meals.

I learned this reaction was a common phenomenon, called food insecurity, among adopted children. It's one of the struggles that adoptive parents face: to teach their children that they will provide enough food, that the kids don't have to overeat or hoard. Many adoptees developed the habit of hiding food not in their tents as the wandering Israelites did, but in their rooms, under their beds or in their toy boxes.

A few months after the Mexican restaurant experience, I took Selam to the park for a picnic. I filled my straw basket with nutritious foods — carrot and celery sticks, apple slices, grapes, a cheese sandwich on multi-grain bread, and yes, a small piece of chocolate for dessert. I reached in and pulled out the carrot and celery sticks as Selam's first course. She grabbed the basket and started riffling through the contents. It was the first time I had witnessed her discriminating tastes; she wanted to choose the food she would eat rather than accepting what I put in front of her.

"No, Selam," I said, taking the chocolate from her hand and replacing it with a carrot stick. "We eat the chocolate for dessert."

Dutifully she ate some carrots and celery, but not all of them. I served her the sandwich, and she tore off the crust and squished it into my hand. After chewing on a bunch of grapes and two apple slices, she was done. A second bunch of grapes and a few more slices of apple remained when she peered in the basket and looked questioningly back at me, seeking permission to remove the dessert.

"You can eat the chocolate now." For the first time, she hadn't eaten everything available. She was turning into a normal American kid — one who wanted dessert first, who rejected fruits and vegetables for sweets. Was she slowly coming to trust, to know that the grapes and apple slices would be in the basket if she got hungry on the way home?

— ❤ —

Dian arrived a year and a half later. As far as we knew, he hadn't experienced the level of starvation that his sister had endured, but his diet had been almost entirely limited to rice cereal.

"Be careful about giving him too much food at once," the social worker warned Heidi.

His first breakfast with our family was at the sumptuous buffet in our four-star hotel in Nanchang. Heidi and Robin placed a hard-boiled egg and a variety of melons on Dian's plate. He gulped it down and reached toward our plates to try the pastries and fried rice. While he didn't exhibit Selam's tendency to indulge and hoard, he was an eager eater, accepting everything placed before him and often wanting more food.

As the months and years passed, both Selam and Dian became more discerning consumers. She rejected the cauliflower in cream sauce, decided she didn't like broccoli but would eat carrots. Dian loved salad but didn't care for cooked vegetables. When I presented them with artichoke hearts from a jar, they ate them grudgingly.

"I like the ones Dad makes, where we pull off the leaves, dip them in butter and then scrape them with our teeth; then Dad takes off the hairs and gives us the heart," Dian explained.

Developing *bitachon* in the new adults in their lives took even longer than trusting in the availability of food. In the orphanage, Selam had interactions with women only. Because she was adopted before she had words, we had no idea about her early experiences with a father, grandfather or other men in the community. She bonded with Robin only after they spent every day together when Heidi went back to work. While Selam eagerly climbed on my lap the first day we met, she was shy around her grandpa for several months. Slowly, she let him hug and hold her.

Just as we wanted to ensure our new grandkids felt secure about food, we wanted them to trust that we would be there for them and would keep our promises. It was important to honor our word not only for *bitachon*, but also to teach truth. (Truth is another *middah*, discussed in the chapter beginning on page 63.) As Rabbi Zeira says in the Talmud (Sukkah 46b), "A person should not say to a child: I will give you something, and then not give it to him, because he thereby comes to teach him about lying."

So when the kids asked about our Friday adventures, I was careful not to make promises unless I was certain I could keep them.

"Can we come back to Heritage Square next Friday?" Selam asked after a day at the amusement park.

"It's pretty expensive; we can come once a month."

Three weeks later, Salam asked, "We went to Heritage Square in June. It's already July. Can we go this Friday?"

I checked the weather forecast. "Looks like it will be a nice day. If it's not raining, we can go back to Heritage Square." And so we did.

"Can we go to the aquarium next Friday?"

"No, Poo and I have tickets to a concert downtown that night, and I don't want to drive so far twice in one day. Let's plan that for next week." And so we did.

"Can we spend the night next week?" Selam asked.

I said "yes" and then came down with a cold. Rather than cancelling, we postponed the sleepover by one night to honor my pledge while minimizing exposure to my germs.

From what we planned to do each Friday to what I vowed to make for lunch — most often mac and cheese — I attempted to keep promises in an effort to build trust and reinforce honesty.

Building *bitachon* that we would not abandon them also remained an ongoing test. When Selam was seven, I took a three-week safari to Africa, missing my weekly volunteering in her classroom. After I returned, I joined the family at the pool, and she ignored me. At the end of our swim she said, "Don't come to my class on Tuesday. I don't want you there."

I was hurt and confused. She had always eagerly welcomed me in her classroom; now I was being rejected. I visited her family at home every Sunday, trying to re-establish our connection. After about a month, Selam said, "My friend Jon wants you to come back to our class." I returned to my regular Tuesday visits.

As I reflected on this interaction, I wondered whether my prolonged absence had jeopardized her trust. Perhaps she had decided to abandon me before I had a chance to abandon her again. I had to prove I would be there for her before she was ready to readmit me into her life.

I thought about my own childhood experiences with *bitachon*. I had never experienced hunger. While my mother wasn't a creative or inspired cook — brisket on Mondays, chicken on Tuesdays, meatballs and spaghetti on Wednesdays, filet of sole on Thursdays and chicken again on Fridays — there was always plenty to eat. Trust in people and in God, however, was more difficult for me.

My father was a powder keg, always on the verge of eruption. We never knew when or who would be caught in the outburst, but we could trust there would be a blow-up almost daily.

"Wash up, it's time for dinner," my mother said. Knowing that I had to pass inspection, I scoured my hands, but it wasn't good enough.

"Your fingernails are awful. Cleanliness is next to godliness. Go wash again," Dad hollered as I picked up my fork. I skulked from the room to re-scrub my nails.

Through these nightly dramas, I feared not only my father but the omnipotent, revengeful God that my parents evoked. When I dared to act out before my father came home from work, Mom's refrain was "God will punish you." Rather than "in God we trust" it was "in God I fear."

As a teenager, I rejected this punitive Supreme Being and traded fear for hope that God would come to my aid. When my adolescent angst led to sleepless nights, I talked to God as my counselor to help me navigate through my shy, awkward attempts with boys, and as my fairy godmother to make my dreams come true. As I tossed and turned, I petitioned:

"Please God; let Martin accept my invitation to the Friday night dance." Alas, it didn't work. After I found the courage to call this handsome boy in my biology class, he said he had other plans.

I tried again. "Please God, let me get an A on the chemistry test." Better luck with this request. Of course the hours of late night study didn't hurt.

In college, I rejected God altogether as I studied philosophy and we tackled the question, "Is there a God?" Instead of *bitachon*, I tried to apply logic, and it failed me. As Rabbi Harry Zeitlin contends, "Judaism is entirely based on trust. We're asked to validate experiences of that which we cannot perceive. Although semi-proofs, lacking all rigor, are easy to find, in truth it's impossible to prove God's existence. . . ."

For many years, I lacked that trust. I performed the rituals of my religion — lighting Chanukah candles, hosting a Passover *seder* dinner — without a belief system. I began to yearn for a greater connection.

"Judaism has a tenacious ability to lie dormant for many years in the recesses of our memory and then suddenly move to the forefront of our consciousness. . . .Whatever the spark, suddenly a portal opens and we catch a glimpse of Judaism that is meaningful, relevant and accessible," writes Rabbi Jamie Korngold.

I found relevant Judaism at Congregation Beth Evergreen. I met like-minded Jews, transplants from the East and West coasts, who had rejected the restrictive, rule-bound Judaism of their childhoods as I had. I attended Friday night services where Rabbi Jamie and the band played liturgy set to the music of the Grateful Dead and James Taylor, and I sang along with a feeling of joy I had never before experienced at synagogue. I began studying and practicing *Mussar* with new friends. I participated in social action projects at the nearby senior center. Yet I still had to wrestle with my concepts of God and of trust.

Once again, my grandchildren provided guidance as I reflected on how their *bitachon* had evolved. First, like the Israelites in the desert, they learned to trust that their basic need for food would be met. Later they developed confidence that they could depend on our family and feel safe in the world. As Selam and Dian moved from fear to believing in what Rabbi David Jaffe calls "the goodness of the universe," I traveled with them.

If my grandchildren could find bitachon despite their early traumas, perhaps I could relinquish some of my worry and anxiety, trusting in a source of strength larger than myself.

Journal prompts

- When have you experienced lack of trust?
- How do you move from worry to *bitachon*?
- What are ways that you can practice building trust through small choices?

Enthusiasm — *Zerizut*

"The word "enthusiasm" comes from the Greek word "entheos," which means the God within. And the happiest, most interesting people are those who have found the secret of maintaining their enthusiasm, that God within."

— Earl Nightingale

When I left a writing workshop one evening, I felt renewed enthusiasm to continue working on a chapter for my book. I got in the car eager to get home to my computer. First I turned on my cell phone and found a voice mail:

"Hi. This is Selam, and you need to call me back instantly. We just went out to the sushi restaurant from the coupon you gave us. And we chowed and chowed and chowed just like always. It was sooo good." Her voice rushed over the airways, breathless with *zerizut*.

I recalled other animated voice mails from my seven-year-old granddaughter over the past few weeks:

"This is Selam and we are home from the hot springs and I got to hold a baby in the big pool. And she was only four months old. And she threw up but not when I was holding her; she threw up when her dad was holding her. And I made a new friend, and her mother made a yummy smoothie, and it had kale and spinach and strawberries and almond milk and that's all. And can we make a concoction like that when we come to your house on Friday?"

"Hi. This is Selam. Where are you? Why aren't you home? I need to talk to you. The butterflies came out of their chrysalis, and they all flew away, but there's one still in the chrysalis, and maybe it will come out of its shell tomorrow."

And a text message, words intermingled with emojis of horses, happy faces and thumbs up:

"Hello I got to ride two horses today. I got to ride one with a saddle, and I didn't fall off, and the other one I rode without the saddle, and I almost fell off. I slid on its back. And where are you and what are you doing now? And where are you taking us on Friday?"

Selam and Dian arrived at our house that Friday morning — the last one they would spend with us before going back to school — ready for a big adventure.

"What are we doing today?" Dian asked.

"Remember when we went to the county fair last year and you got to pet the rabbits? Do you want to go today?"

"*Yes*! Let's leave right now," Selam enthused.

"It doesn't open for a couple of hours. You can help me get ready." Selam filled water bottles with ice while Dian packed plastic snack bags with cheddar cheese bunnies, popcorn and blueberries.

We arrived shortly before the fair opened, and Selam jumped out of the car and dashed across the grass to the entrance. She ran back and forth across the covered walkway, finding a map of the fair as we waited with the crowd of other eager kids and their families.

"Let's go," she shouted as she spotted the guard collecting tickets.

"Where should we go first?" I asked as I studied the map.

They answered by dashing toward a two-story metal tower spewing giant translucent bubbles.

"Look, I got one," Selam said, smashing the enormous sphere with her hands as Dian stomped one under his feet. Other kids joined, and it was a race to see who could burst the most bubbles before they landed on the grass. After ten minutes, we were ready to move on.

"Let's go inside and see the Kidz Science Safari," I suggested.

The kids squinted, adjusting to the dim light of the dirt floor barn, transformed for the weekend into a science laboratory. Dian, drawn to the stationary bike with a mounted light, jumped on the seat and began pedaling.

"Look, Moo, the faster you go, the brighter the light gets." He slowed down to a crawl and the light dimmed. He stopped; the bulb went out. He sped up again; the light got brighter. Magic!

Selam stopped across the room, fascinated by a machine spewing air, a red ball suspended above. Looking down on the floor beneath the contraption, she spotted green and yellow balls, grabbed them and figured out how to make them dance in the air alongside the red one.

"Let's see what else is at the fair," Selam said after they made their way around the semi-circle of science exhibits — a Tesla machine, wind tunnels and a giant light box with brightly colored pegs.

Outside on a small stage in the plaza, a magician in a top hat entertained a group of families gathered on the lawn as he transformed a dollar bill into a hundred, then back again.

"Let's watch," Selam said, plopping down in the grass. Dian and I joined her.

"I need a volunteer for this next trick," Magician Dave announced. Without hesitation, Selam's hands darted up, her bottom springing off the ground as she oohed to get Dave's attention.

Her enthusiasm brought to mind the biblical Rebekah, whom Mussar teachers cite as a model of *zerizut* — someone who acted with alacrity when called to be a helper. Rebekah hastened to provide water not only for Abraham's servant but also for his camels, and thereby was deemed a suitable bride for Isaac.

"I need a volunteer who looks just like . . . you," Dave said, surveying the audience before pointing at Selam.

She jumped up, her face beaming with delight.

"What's your name?" the magician asked.

"Selam."

"Wave to the audience, Selam."

Selam lifted her arms and brandished them in the air as the crowd cheered. I thought back to the bashful five-year-old who had left the stage during her first dance recital. After entering from backstage and spotting the room filled with parents and grandparents, her shyness had triumphed over enthusiasm. Despite the cajoling of her teachers and grandparents, she sat down on the edge of the stage and refused to budge. Now, three years later, she was up on another stage, the only child, soaking in the attention of an even larger crowd.

"Hold the two ends of this rope," Dave instructed as he handed Selam a long nylon cord. "Cutting off the ends makes this rope magical."

He snipped, leaving two small white strings in Selam's hands. She stared, entranced, as Dave performed the time-worn "cut and restore" rope trick, making two pieces, then three, and lastly restoring the rope to its original intact state.

"Let's thank Selam for her help," Dave said.

The audience applauded as Selam skipped back to her place on the grass. "I helped him do magic!" She opened her clasped hand, presenting the two short pieces of twine — her souvenir of *zerizut*.

"Wow. What? How's he doing that?" The usually reserved Dian leapt up and shouted as the magician performed his next trick with silver linking Chinese rings. Parents in the crowd turned toward Dian, smiling and laughing at his unbridled joy.

The magic show over, the kids headed toward another barn, this one redolent with the telltale aroma of horses. Irv and I trailed behind. As he rounded the corner, Dian spied the tallest horses we had ever seen, the stately black Percherons that would perform later that night in the equestrian acrobatic show. "They are so tall. I've never seen horses this big," he marveled.

The grandkids spotted the outdoor adventure park across the field, where there were kayaks, a climbing wall and dirt bikes. Dian, who had been fearful around water when he first arrived in our family, chose to kayak in the huge pool. He paddled round and round, grinning as he skillfully avoided the other boats.

"You sure were in that pool for a long time. Did you have fun?" I asked him.

"I tried to get out sooner, but there were too many kids in the way. I had to keep going around them to get to the exit," Dian answered, modeling not only the energy, but also the persistence of *zerizut*.

After several hours I said, "It's time to go home for dinner."

"Please, can we see one more thing," Selam begged.

"Let's go see the reptiles as our last stop."

Dian and Selam found front row seats as the Reptile Adventures show got under way.

"I need volunteers to help me hold this next snake," showman Danny announced as he gingerly removed an albino Burmese python from its enormous box.

Once again, Selam's hand darted up, and Danny chose her, along with five other kids, to hold the long, thick, glossy yellow snake. First in line, Selam held Apollo's head, and the others held his body as Danny explained the story of this gentle giant. The python snaked his head around Selam's arms while the showman addressed the audience. While my granddaughter remained calm, focused on the reptile in her hands, I began to fidget in my seat. *The trainer's not paying enough attention to the snake. It's coiling around Selam's arm. This looks a bit dangerous,* I thought. *Has her enthusiasm taken her into unsafe territory?*

My childhood experiences with animals had largely been confined to observing tigers and lions imprisoned behind the black bars of the Prospect Park or Bronx zoos. Today my grandkids had already had numerous animal encounters, but they had all felt safe. They had viewed the Percherons ensconced in stalls with trainers at their sides; they had held pet rabbits while the owners stood close by; and Selam had been led around a small arena on a tethered pony. The little pony had nibbled on Selam's fingers, but she wasn't fazed. Now she was holding the massive head of a wriggling snake.

I allowed and even encouraged her to participate. Was it the right decision? Was this as safe as the other animal adventures? I breathed a sigh of relief as she returned to her seat unscathed.

Before going to the car, we stopped in a nearby building to use the restroom. But wait! There was more to see. The 4-H cake baking contest was on display, as tempting as a Parisian patisserie.

"Look at that white cake. It's in the shape of a dog. It has black eyes and a pink nose!" Selam's fingers inched across the plastic tablecloth toward the yummy looking confection, and then withdrew as I gently placed my hand on top of hers.

"No touching, no tasting," I said, worried that her *zerizut* might cross the boundaries of proper behavior.

"Can I take a picture of the cakes, puh-leeeze." I handed her my cell phone, relieved she was satisfied to photograph rather than sample the enticing desserts. Selam snapped photos in rapid succession as she marveled at the creative delights — a rainbow-decorated layer cake; a lime green frosted cake topped with forest green pine trees and an orange log cabin; and a white cake bedecked with a cowgirl in pink riding boots.

"Can I take a picture of that one?" Dian pleaded, pointing at a chocolate cake topped with bunnies surrounded by a base of pastel ovals reminiscent of Easter eggs. Cakes iced with lemon yellow, fire-engine red and baby blue caught his eye, and he photographed them all.

I gently steered them toward the exit, and they babbled all the way home about what they had seen. Their enthusiasm persisted as they shared their adventures with their dad. "I got to ride a pony!" "I kayaked around a big pool!" "We petted a goat!"

Tired as I was, I went up to my office to capture the excitement of the day by journaling about our adventures. I reflected that my grandkids had modeled two *Mussar* definitions of *zerizut*: acting swiftly and completing the task. Selam had not only raised her hand with enthusiasm, but also had grasped the magic white rope and nestled the squirming snake for as long as the performers had required. Dian, who had overcome his apprehension of water, had taken the risk to kayak and kept going until he found a way out. Once again they had provided a day of memories as well as inspiration for my *Mussar* practice.

Journal prompts
- Who are your models/teachers for *zerizut*? Why?
- When do you act with alacrity and intention?
- What are obstacles (fear, exhaustion) that create resistance to starting and completing a task?

Compassion — *Rachamim*

"Compassion is to sense another person's existence, understand his thinking and feelings, connect to him, and to realize that the connection itself is the goal."

— Rabbi Itamar Schwartz

Three years of kidney dialysis had taken its toll on my mother. She needed a walker to get around even in her small house. Her head drooped, and she fell asleep as she tried to read a Janet Evanovich mystery or watch her favorite television show, *Family Feud*. She ate three tablespoons of cereal for breakfast and two bites of tuna salad for lunch.

Her ninety-year-old body couldn't withstand much more as she struggled with fatigue and fluid in her lungs. She had been a fighter; her urologist called her the "Energizer Bunny." But now her spirit, her energy and her body were failing.

In January, she had fallen off the kitchen chair while reaching for her pills. I flew down to Florida from Colorado. Layers of paper-thin white blankets cloaked her frail body in the austere, aluminum-framed hospital bed. She seemed to be disappearing before my eyes. She could hardly lift her head off the pillow to greet me. Through tear-veiled eyes, I gaped at this woman who had birthed me and nurtured me for more than six decades.

"She had a really bad night last night," her hospital roommate said. "She was unsettled, groaning, tossing and turning, and calling out for help." The doctor said Mom's lungs were filled with fluid, her brain was oxygen deficient, and she moved in and out of lucidity. *The end has come,* I thought.

Once again, she made a miraculous rebound. Her urologist refused to suspend treatment because he thought he could keep her alive a bit longer. Instead he sent her to a rehab center where she could continue her dialysis while regaining her strength. I returned to Colorado.

A week later, I called Mom on my cell phone from the synagogue parking lot before going into my *Mussar* class.

"Why did you save me? All my friends are able to die. Why can't I? If you save me next time, I'll never talk to you again." *And if I don't save you, you'll never talk to me again.* A paradox. I dared not utter this musing aloud.

She seemed ready to go; was I ready to let her? She wasn't resisting death, but I was.

I would miss hearing her voice on our daily phone conversations, even when we just talked about the Florida humidity or her Tuesday night outing with "the girls" to Arby's. I would yearn for her call to check on our safety during a Colorado blizzard. Who would share my joy when Selam learned to do a somersault and Dian mastered balancing on a bicycle?

My own fears were getting in the way of letting her go. I trembled at the thought of losing her. She believed that when she died, there would be an abyss of nothingness. I wasn't so sure but still feared death. After she passed, I would be the oldest generation, next in line for death in the natural order of things.

I reflected on the irony of the meaning of compassion in Hebrew — *rachamim* — which has the same root as *rechem* — womb. Alan Morinis reminds us that compassion embodies the strong ties of love that a mother feels for the baby she is carrying. And here I was, my mother's firstborn, trying to find the compassion to let her die despite my wish for her to live. The umbilical cord had been cut at birth; now our human connection would be severed.

A few days later, Mom went home from rehab, and I flew back to Florida. My brother, Herb, and I took her to dialysis. The social worker called us into her office and confirmed what we already knew in our hearts but had not accepted.

"It's time to let her go," she said. "Her body can't do this anymore. I recommend that you don't bring her back here."

Mom's experience on the dialysis machine that morning validated the social worker's words. After an hour, Mom's blood pressure plummeted, and the nurses had to take her off the apparatus. They had extracted mere ounces of toxic fluid from her body. Her brain oxygen was low; her thinking cloudy. We knew she could live only a couple of weeks without dialysis. Yet my siblings and I decided this time would be her last on the machine that had both saved and ravaged her body.

Deep down, I knew my mother was ready to die. The conversation with Mom in the synagogue parking lot was not the first about avoiding life-prolonging measures. She had told us years before that if we tried to keep her alive when she was not going to get better, she'd come back to haunt us. Any remaining doubts vanished when the hospice doctor came to visit her at home a couple of days later. Mom had not yet been introduced to the visitor in the white lab coat, but she stared at him and blurted, "I'm not afraid to die, you know."

On Valentine's Day, she spoke on the phone with my grandchildren for the last time. "You better get down here and get your chocolate," she told Selam. The dying ninety-year-old and the exuberant, candy-loving six-year-old in that moment shared the same illusory world view; neither saw the impossibility of the situation.

"Can we go? Please," Selam begged as she held the phone to her ear. Heidi gently explained that they couldn't make the trip. Selam was disappointed, not only because she wouldn't get her sweets, but also because she would not get to spend time with Sampa (my mother's nickname) or me.

I had been in Florida for almost two weeks, and Selam and I missed each other. My days were long and tedious as I sat at my mother's bedside, hearing her call out for her dead sister. Sometimes I lay down beside her, listening to her shallow breath and holding her hand. My right shoulder began to ache and then throb, my emotional state manifesting in physical pain.

One morning the nurse encouraged me to get outside. "I'll call you on your cell if anything changes."

I walked out the front door and turned automatically toward the nearby park where I could watch the ducks floating along the canal. It was a stroll I had taken with Mom countless times over the decades. My sore shoulder heaved at the thought that she never again would walk this way with me. She was on a different path now. Alone with my thoughts, I reflected on the true meaning of compassion: to surrender my own needs and be truly present to my mother's.

"Compassion allows us to bear witness to suffering, whether it is in ourselves or others, without fear; it allows us to name injustice without hesitation, to act strongly, with all the skill at our disposal," says author and meditation coach Sharon Salzberg.

I am not waiting for her to die, I am waiting with her to die, I thought. With a new appreciation of my role, I went back to her bedside and whispered in her ear, "It's OK. We'll be fine. You can go."

Mom stopped eating and barely opened her eyes. She tossed and turned, moaned and flailed her arms. Early on a Thursday morning, ten days after we had stopped dialysis, the hospice nurse woke my brother, sister and me.

"The time has come," she whispered gently. We scrambled to Mom's side and held her as she took her final breath.

My heart and body ached, yet I was so grateful that I had been there for her transition, and we could honor her wish of dying at home. Putting aside our grief, we swiftly made the phone calls needed to arrange her final flight to New York to be buried next to our father.

After a grueling two months, three trips to Florida and a final goodbye in New York, I couldn't wait to get home. I ached for the hugs of my grandkids.

Before my last trip, Selam had complained, "Why do you have to keep going to Florida?"

"Sampa is very, very sick. I want to see her now as much as possible because when she dies, I will really miss her. I won't be able to talk to her anymore, so I need to be with her now."

Selam and Dian had some experience with death. Their first dog, Blu, had died the year before, and the family had buried him on their property. They drew some pictures to place in the grave and surrounded the site with painted stones. "Blu's up in the sky now," Dian had told me.

So when I talked about missing my mother, Selam was ready with an answer. She looked me in the eye and said, "You will be able to talk to her. Here's how you will do it: First close your eyes. Then say in your head, when no one else is around — Sampa, Sampa, come Sampa. I need to talk to you; appear, appear. I need a hug, Your Majesty."

Selam's words of compassion echoed often in my head through Mom's final days. I managed to choke out the words at the funeral, and used them as a salve in the ensuing days.

When I arrived home and saw Selam and Dian for the first time, they surrounded me with hugs. "Don't be sad. We love you, Moo," Dian said. "Come play with us."

I dreaded the arrival of Mother's Day, barely three months after Mom's death. As I awoke to the bright Colorado sunshine streaming through the bedroom window, my first thought was of Mom. It felt like a stack of bricks was sitting on my chest; my shoulder ached, and my unbidden tears shrouded the mountain view.

Taking a few deep breaths, I tried Selam's suggestion, reclosing my eyes and calling for my mother. I pictured her, radiant in the gold suit she wore to her ninetieth birthday party. My tears came harder and faster as the sharp pain of loss surged through my body. After what seemed like hours, my grief spent, I swung my feet onto the floor and girded myself to face the day. *We're going to see the grandkids.* I comforted myself. *That's always a good distraction.*

A few hours later, encircled by my grandchildren, I felt a bit better. After playing on the swings, we gathered around the dinner table for

Robin's gourmet Mother's Day meal of surf and turf — salmon and cooked-to-perfection tenderloin.

The conversation turned to height. Selam, one of the tallest in her class, predicted that she would be taller than me, her five-foot grandma, by the time she was ten.

"Probably true since you're already at my shoulder," I agreed. "I come from a family of short women, and your family was tall."

"Sampa was the shortest one of all," Selam said.

"But she's dead now," Dian stated in a matter-of-fact tone. In the shocked silence, pain struck me in my gut.

But then Selam retorted, "Don't rub it in."

We broke into laughter. We had never heard her use that expression before, and yet it was a lighthearted application of a well-worn phrase.

I remembered how many times this tough, often bossy granddaughter had expressed compassion. Even before she had words, she showed connection to others in pain. Perhaps because she had come from an orphanage filled with crying babies, Selam reacted instinctively when she heard a child sobbing.

Three hours into a plane trip, a two-year-old sitting across the aisle started fussing. Selam, five at the time, immediately reached over to show him her well-worn, well-loved, fuzzy brown teddy bear.

"I want to sit with him. Can you tell his mom about my experience holding kids?" Selam asked Heidi. "Maybe I can trade seats with his dad." Minutes later, she and the toddler were giggling as they played hide-and-seek behind their hands. The rest of the trip passed smoothly as the two entertained each other.

Later at baggage claim, Selam's exhausted new friend was throwing a temper tantrum while our travel-weary families crammed around the carousel waiting for the slow-moving machine to belch out our luggage. Selam again came to the rescue. Without a word, she drew close to him and started rubbing his back. He looked up and smiled through his tears at his newfound ally.

Dian, quite a bit more reserved, kept his compassion closer to home and often came unbidden when he somehow sensed that I needed support. One evening, I was alone in the kitchen cooking dinner for company while Heidi chatted with one guest and Selam played chess with another. I was feeling a bit put-upon, bearing the full weight of meal prep as the others socialized.

I looked up from stirring the rice to find Dian was at my side. "I want to help you, Moo." He opened the cutlery drawer and counted out seven each of knives, forks and spoons to set the table. Dian had instinctively come to the rescue, just by being present for me, which was exactly what I needed at that moment.

Had I done the same for others? I wondered. I remembered being disappointed when an ailing friend rejected my offer to deliver homemade brownies, only to learn he was a diabetic. Compassionate? Not so much. On the other hand, when I provided Passover leftovers to a friend undergoing chemo, she was delighted to get the jarred gefilte fish that was so much a part of our tradition. It wasn't necessarily about the time taken to prepare the food, it was about giving the friend what would most resonate. *Rachamim was rather simple if I could get myself out of the way and care enough to stand in the other person's shoes.*

Through their actions, Selam and Dian had provided a twist on l'*dor vador*, defined as the responsibility to transmit spiritual and cultural traditions from one generation to the next. I was learning the *middah* of *rachamim* from the generations that came before — and after — me. My dying mother had helped me move past my fear of losing her, so I could accompany her with compassion on her final journey. And my grandchildren had modeled *rachamim* through their instinctive reactions to the needs of others — whether it was a crying child at baggage claim or an abandoned hostess feeling forlorn in the kitchen.

Journal prompts
- When is it appropriate to express *rachamim* through humor?
- When have you felt deep compassion and how did it impact you?
- What gets in the way of feeling and showing compassion to others?

Truth, Honesty — *Emet*

"Before you tell a truth that can cause only pain and inflict gratuitous hurt, ask yourself why you should tell it. There are indeed times when a pretty lie is preferable to an ugly truth."

— Rabbi Joseph Telushkin

"Moo, your belly is fat. Is there a baby in there?" Five-year-old Selam extended her index finger with its peeling red nail polish and pointed at my protruding stomach. We were standing naked in the communal shower at the Bailey pool as we washed the chlorine out of our hair and off our skin. We had just spent a fun-filled hour of chasing each other, taking turns being the shark under water.

I frowned. Unlike my tummy, my spirits deflated as I faced an unbidden, unwelcome truth. Indeed, I contemplated with regret, the naked reality was that I no longer had the flat abs of a thirty-year-old. No matter how many stomach crunches I repeated or Nestle Crunches I avoided, my figure had changed. Glancing down, suddenly self-conscious, I finished rinsing my aging body and grabbed my brown terry cloth towel off the nearby hook, tightly wrapping and concealing my sagging breasts, paunchy tummy and bruised ego.

"No baby in there, Selam. That's just my tummy."

Should I tell her that her comments hurt my feelings? Young kids don't have the same filters that adults do. I was faced with a dilemma. I didn't think she was being mean; she was acting out of curiosity. Perhaps the last big-tummied woman in the communal shower actually did have a "baby in there." I made the choice to say nothing this time.

The question of *emet* resurfaced during another family outing a few weeks later. We had spent the day at the aquarium, watching the mermaids dive, the tigers pace and the otters frolic. When we arrived at the car, the kids got in first while I helped Irv lift his electric scooter into the trunk.

The taste of the fish taco I had eaten in the aquarium restaurant fouled my mouth. No toothbrush handy, I reached into the car's center console to grab a stick of gum. I couldn't find it.

"Anyone know what happened to the Trident? I was sure there was some in here." I riffled through the hodgepodge of items — hand sanitizer, a granola bar, tissues, deodorant, earphones and a phone charging cord. No gum.

"I didn't take it," Selam piped up.

"I didn't take it," Dian echoed.

"Hmm. I was sure there was gum in here. I wonder what happened to it."

"We don't know," came the chorus from the back seat.

A few minutes later, I was driving on the interstate headed toward the Walmart that was going out of business. I had promised each kid a half-priced toy. I glanced in the rearview mirror at the unusually quiet grandkids. Both were chewing.

"Are you chewing gum? Where did you get it?"

Without answering, Selam reached forward, stretching the seatbelt that harnessed her in her booster seat.

"Here, Poo," she said, handing a package of Trident to her grandpa.

"You both lied to me. I'm disappointed. We are going straight home. No new toys today." I zoomed past the exit and kept heading west, stewing about their dishonesty. I remembered previous unpleasant car rides where I had to warn the kids about the consequences of bad behavior like fighting and lying.

One morning as we headed to the zoo, I looked through the rearview mirror and saw Dian pouting.

"She's bugging me," Dian said.

"Move over to your side and stop touching Dian," I told Selam.

"He touched me first."

"She started it. She grabbed my water bottle," Dian whined.

And so it went, round and round. Who was telling the truth? Without a video recording of the incident, I would never know.

This time, however, I was rankled because rather than lying about each other's responsibility for a tiff, Selam and Dian had colluded in a lie. So the dishonesty seemed more egregious.

I reflected that children's lying to protect themselves was as common as their blurting out what they thought. I would have welcomed a white lie, or no comment at all, when Selam stared at my nude body. Lying about the gum, though, was not appreciated.

It made me wonder when, if ever, it is permissible to lie: Is it about the circumstances? Is it about intention — lying to protect the other versus lying to protect oneself? Or is it more about the impact of the falsehood?

I did some research into what Jewish law had to say about lying and found that, by and large, dishonesty and deceit are serious crimes. Yet there are circumstances when it is encouraged, even required: to keep the peace, to avoid hurting another person's feelings or to provide comfort. "Given the choice, when it came to interpersonal relations, the sages valued peace over truth," Rabbi Lord Jonathan Sacks says.

An oft-quoted example of honesty in Jewish theology is the argument between the schools of Hillel and Shammai, two illustrious sages of the first century, as to what to say about the bride at a wedding. The custom was to say, "The bride is beautiful and graceful."

Members of the school of Shammai thought it was improper to utter these words if they did not believe them to be true. The school of Hillel took a different view. After all, wasn't it the groom who judged the bride's beauty, not some external, objective standard? So praising the bride endorsed the groom's choice and celebrated the marriage. Therefore, the school of Hillel asserted it was OK to say the bride was beautiful in all circumstances.

As a person who valued relationship over *emet*, I more often sided with Hillel. I thought about my less-than-honest response when a friend gave me a pearl necklace that I didn't like. I didn't want to hurt her feelings by asking if I could exchange it. Instead, I accepted the gift with profuse thanks, immediately fastened the clasp around my neck, and wore it the next time we went to lunch. I never wore it again. It sat in my jewelry box for years until I gave it to Selam.

I distinguished between telling the truth when it's helpful and not when it hurts. When I shopped with my friend for a New Year's Eve outfit, I advised frankly which dress was the most becoming and which didn't flatter her figure. But when she came to a party in an uncomplimentary blouse, I said nothing. She had already purchased it; the truth wouldn't be useful.

I reflected on the intricacies of truth. Sometimes the most difficult truth is being honest with and about myself. Learning *Mussar*, I began practicing self-honesty by journaling and meditating about how my actions affected others.

During the High Holidays, the Jewish New Year, I decided to observe the ritual of *taschlich*, casting away my sins. I took a few slices of bread and drove to the fast-flowing waters of the South Platte River. Recalling my wrongdoings of the past year, I tore the bread into small pieces, each representing a sin, and tossed them into the river. It was a singular opportunity to right any wrongs and start with a clean slate.

The grandkids came to visit after I returned from the river, and I explained that I had used bread to symbolize and discard my sins.

"What are sins? What do you mean?" Selam asked.

I remembered when the kids lied about taking the gum from my car console. "For example, you might ask for forgiveness for taking my Trident without permission and lying about it," I suggested. Selam sat in silence, pondering.

"I know, I can throw bread in the water about my pouting," Dian chimed in.

"That's a good idea," Heidi replied. Dian often expressed his unspoken needs with an annoying whine and an unhappy facial expression rather than stating what he wanted. And his mother's frustrated refrain was, "Stop pouting and tell me what you want."

After making his declaration, Dian quickly added, "But I'll probably pout again next year." We all chuckled at his humble honesty.

"And I'll probably be impatient again. That's something I have to work on all the time. We ask for forgiveness to think about what we can do better next year and get another chance. None of us will be perfect," I said.

I thought about the lessons presented by the grandkids' truths (a protruding tummy, the inability to stop pouting) and a lie (stolen gum). Selam's observation about my tummy continued to reverberate. When I caught an unwelcome glimpse of my profile, I remembered her words and swore off chocolate chip cookies, at least for that day.

Then I decided to use my bulging tummy as a metaphor. I might not evade a swelling stomach, but I could strive to avoid bloated words and white lies. Rather than exaggerating: "I told you a million times I get sick from hot dogs," I could say, "I had a bad experience with hot dogs as a kid, and I still don't eat them." It was a small distinction perhaps, but one that led to a path of truth-telling rather than down the slippery slope toward lying.

The grandkids' lie about taking the gum reminded me that both adults and children lie for self-protection. Could I be more mindful and distinguish between when I lied not to shield the other, but to protect myself? I looked for *bechirah* points as opportunities for truth-telling. When snow threatened, I dreaded the early morning drive down the mountain for a volunteer commitment. Rather than my habitual, "I *can't* make the meeting," I simply said, "I *won't* make the meeting." It was another small, yet significant opportunity to avoid a white lie and grow my soul.

Dian's truth about casting away his "sin" of pouting was a lesson in accepting the truth of my own imperfections and, perhaps more importantly, understanding that my faults are not the whole of who I am. Too often in the past, I had focused on my shortcomings rather than on my spiritual journey. Through the practice of *Mussar*, I began to make more mindful choices, to celebrate successes and to view setbacks as opportunities for learning. For example, as I practiced mindfulness and became more aware of impatience triggers, like waiting in long grocery lines or driving in stop-and-go traffic, I more often chose to take a deep breath. At the same time, I accepted that there would be instances where I would tap my foot and feel my body tense with irritation. *Mussar*, I reminded myself, *is a lifelong journey.*

Journal prompts
- When have you lied to others to safeguard them?
- When have you lied to others to protect yourself?
- When has a friend's radical honesty helped you face a truth you've avoided?

Humility — *Anavah*

"The practice of humility requires us to view each person we encounter as our teacher and to struggle to learn something from each person."
— Rabbi Ira Stone

I was running a little late to Mrs. B's second grade classroom, so the students were already in reading groups when I got there. Mrs. B. had gathered the kids in the purple group around the semi-circular table at the back of the classroom to discuss what they had read and check for comprehension. The students in the orange group sprawled across the brightly colored carpet as they read silently.

The kids in the blue and green groups were supposed to be in their seats around the square tables, working individually on vocabulary exercises in their *Spelling Connections* workbook. A handful of the students were already on task; the rest had yet to settle down and wandered around the classroom. They were crawling under the table to retrieve workbooks, sharpening pencils or chatting with their neighbors. Isaac ran over and gave me hug.

"I knew you were coming today because it's Tuesday," he said, his cornflower blue eyes shining up at me as his arms encircled my waist. Lee joined us. "I thought you were Dian's grandma. Why are you hugging Isaac?"

"I am Dian's grandma, and Isaac and the other kids are my friends too," I answered, humbled by the love and attention of these seven-year-olds, who would be my teachers this day.

I sat down beside Isaac and Dian and coaxed them to open the shiny, cherry red cover of their spelling books. They riffled through their cluttered desk drawers in search of spiral spelling notebooks. After extracting erasers, glue sticks and crumbled worksheets, they finally unearthed the buried notebooks and opened to a blank page.

The workbook exercise required students to fill in the blank of a rhyme with one of their spelling words. The first question: "A clown will be riding (she doesn't need fuel). She'll come into town on the back of a _____. "

"Wave!" Isaac shouted without hesitation.

"Hmm. That would be a good answer. A clown might ride in on a wave. But it has to rhyme with fuel. Is there another spelling word that might work better?"

In the past, as a teacher or a parent helping with homework, I would have jumped in with the right answer. Today I decided to "take up the right amount of space," Morinis' definition of *anavah*, and not snatch the student's opportunity to succeed on his own.

So rather than providing the answer, I waited in silence as Isaac perused the list of spelling words at the top of the page.

"I get it, *mule*," he blurted after a few seconds.

"That's the one." I smiled as I high-fived him, delighted in his joy and pleased I hadn't stolen his chance to solve the problem himself.

Later, volunteering in Selam's third grade class I worked with Diego on an exercise in their version of *Spelling Connections*. We sat in the back of the room huddled together, speaking softly as the rest of the class worked individually at their desks. This lesson was a bit more sophisticated. In a style suggestive of the TV show *Jeopardy*, the exercise provided a definition, and the students had to choose the spelling word that best fit.

We were going along at a quick clip when we came to "something that turns" as the meaning.

"A stream?" Diego asked as his index finger moved down the list of spelling words.

"That's a very creative answer. Streams certainly make turns. Is there another word that might also work?" Again, I vowed to remain silent and give the student room for discovery.

Diego continued down the list, his mouth moving as he sounded out the words. He was a bit confused because he thought he had already found the answer.

"Is it wheel?"

"I think so," I replied, reflecting not only at the creativity of this eight-year-old, but also how the writer of the text hadn't taken into account the possibility of "stream" as an answer. Diego's first choice would have been marked as incorrect on a multiple-choice test.

Growing up in New York, where we had annual state exams, I had learned to be an excellent test taker and prided myself in finding the "right" answer. Now second and third graders were teaching me a lesson in humility, that the test designer's right answer wasn't always the only, or even the most creative one.

After about ten minutes, Mrs. M. called the third graders back together to check their work. Diego gathered up his completed worksheet and workbook, and walked back to his seat as I observed from the back of the room. When the teacher asked for volunteers to provide the answers, Selam's hand waved wildly. She was one of a dozen students eager to answer every question.

I beamed with pride as the teacher called on Selam, and she answered the question correctly. I noticed that Diego remained quiet, his hands folded in his lap, even though he and I had finished the work together, and he had all the answers. *Is he too shy to participate or too unsure of himself? He certainly isn't taking up any space,* I thought.

Watching these third graders brought me back to Mrs. Siegel's crowded junior high classroom in Brooklyn. The more extroverted, quick-witted students got all the attention, both from the teachers and fellow students. I wasn't one of them.

One day Mrs. Siegel read the Sir Francis Bacon quote, "Some books should be tasted, some devoured, but only a few should be chewed and digested thoroughly." And then she asked, "Which books should be digested?"

Steve, a class clown, shouted out, "The small ones."

The entire class roared, including Mrs. Siegel. Rather than being reprimanded for not raising his hand, Steve earned another notch in his Mr. Popularity belt. I never would have dreamed of calling out a wisecrack in class. I was the quiet girl in the last row. At that moment though, as Steve basked in the attention, I wished I had been the funny, outgoing kid who had the chutzpah to reveal her wit.

How come it's OK for the popular boys to shout out, but not for the diligent girls? I wondered. For some reason, the incident stayed with me for decades. It didn't change my behavior; I never quipped aloud in class. But it did make me think about "taking up the right amount of space" long before I had the *Mussar* language to explain it. The boys in the class, like Steve, were comfortable taking up more space while I was on the other side of the humility scale, sitting shyly in the back of the room and avoiding notice.

As I grew older, however, I began to assume a subtle leadership role. Because I was dependable, my teachers encouraged me to run for class treasurer and serve as newspaper editor. As an adult, I worked hard on volunteer boards and became an unexpected leader as president of our synagogue and other nonprofit groups.

When I had considered *anavah* as a synonym for being shy and quiet, I thought I had that *middah* nailed. Not only was I reserved at school, but also in my childhood home. It was a survival technique. I was adept at avoiding the attention that came with the ever-present danger of arousing my father's temper.

When I applied the *Mussar* definition of humility, taking up the right amount of space, I discovered I had lots of room to grow this soul trait in my professional and personal lives. Could I learn to take up the right amount of space for the situation, finding the balance between self-effacement and arrogance?

There were times that I didn't have the self-confidence to take an appropriate role. When my professional organization was planning an event, I sat silently and let the more assertive members prevail even though I had useful information that might have added to the discussion. *Why didn't I share my knowledge about the venue and maybe help our group avoid some problems?* I thought later.

Other times, I wanted recognition. *That was my idea! I proposed it first!* I pouted when the committee ignored my suggestion to bring in a guest speaker, only to enthusiastically support it when a man mentioned the same idea minutes later.

On the other side of the humility scale, I took up too much space by finishing the sentences of friends who talked too slowly or deliberately from my New York point of view.

"I don't want to go to the party because . . . ," my friend hesitated.

"I know you're tired from watching your grandkids," I finished.

"No, I don't want to go because I have an early meeting the next morning," my friend answered, exasperated that I had jumped in with an incorrect assumption.

As a grandma, I had the opportunity to learn how to take up only my rightful place in yet another setting. By being patient and treating every child as my teacher, I was practicing humility when I volunteered in the classroom.

I also applied taking up the right amount of space as the grandmother and not the parent. The dent in my tongue from biting back unbidden advice grew deeper as I watched my daughter as mother.

"You can't have dessert unless you finish all the food on your plate. Eat your kale," Heidi cajoled. Selam, who as a toddler had eaten everything in sight and begged for more, had become as fussy as any other American eight-year-old. Now she was being forced to eat all her green vegetables.

I silently cringed, remembering how my parents had made me eat every last morsel because "the children in India are starving." As a result, I had spent my entire adult life fighting the ingrained habit of cleaning my plate even when I was already satiated. Rebelling against my upbringing, I did not adhere to the "clean your plate" philosophy when raising my kids. I encouraged, but didn't force them, to eat their vegetables. My daughter had adopted a philosophy closer to my parents'. I kept quiet.

She is the parent, better not interfere, I thought. *I can use it as a lesson in humility — my parents did it one way; I did it another; my daughter has her way. After all, who knows the best way to raise healthy eaters and who am I to judge?*

I learned that *anavah* was a worthy *middah* for my practice. Being mindful, I recognized that sometimes I took up too much space, jumping in to solve a problem, finish a sentence or provide advice. Other times, I made myself invisible, sitting quietly instead of sharing valuable information.

How could I make the appropriate choice for the circumstance and take up my rightful space? I considered the *anavah* advice of Rabbi Simcha Bunim, eighteenth century Hasidic master, "Everyone must have two pockets, so that he can reach into the one or the other, according to his needs. In his right pocket are to be the words: 'For my sake was the world created,' and in his left: 'I am but dust and ashes.'"

My challenge was to determine which piece of paper to metaphorically take out of my pocket in any given situation.

Journal prompts
- Who has been your unexpected teacher?
- In what circumstances do you take up too much space? Too little space?
- What gets in your way of taking up the right amount of space?

Responsibility — *Achrayut*

"In the long run, we shape our lives, and we shape ourselves. The process never ends until we die. And the choices we make are ultimately our own responsibility."

— Eleanor Roosevelt

I was sitting at my desk when the phone rang. The caller ID displayed Heidi's home number. I picked up the receiver and was rewarded with the sweet sound of my granddaughter's voice. Hearing her on the other end of the line, I felt a surge of love and gratitude washing over my body like warm, salty waves at Brighton Beach on an August day.

"Hi Moo. Where is my coat?" she asked, getting right down to business. None of her regular conversation starters: "What are you doing? How was your day?"

"Your coat? Are you missing a coat?"

"Yes, my pink and gray one. I can't find it."

"Do you think you left it at my house? Let me go look in my car, but I haven't seen it there."

Holding the cordless phone against my ear, I reported my progress as I went down the stairs, opened the garage door, turned on the light and started searching my Toyota. I moved the Natural Grocers bags filled with exercise and swimming attire, the yoga mat, my hiking pack and assorted other items stored in my trunk, all to no avail. I searched between the booster seats and on the floor.

"No coat in my car. When's the last time you saw it?"

"I think it was Friday." Her voice was low and flat; she was worried.

I thought back to Friday. It had been a chaotic afternoon at school with Halloween parties in the classrooms. Selam had changed into her witch costume with its frilly black-fringed dress and pointed, wide-brimmed hat, accessorized with shiny black patent leather mini-heels, before I had arrived in her classroom. So I did not know where she had stored her street clothes.

As we got ready to leave the school after the parties, I was weighed down with two cumbersome pumpkins. I felt them slipping out of my arms. I had decorated them with skewers of fruit and cheese to fulfill my grandmotherly obligation of a healthful snack. The skewers were gone, but carrying the pumpkins made my shoulders ache. Worse yet, exiting families packed the hallways, and I struggled to avoid bumping into others. Irv was having trouble staying upright. He was leaning hard on his walking stick because his new prosthetic foot was hurting. For everyone's sake, I was eager to get to the car.

Just feet from the exit, Selam stopped short, "My shoes!"

"We'll wait here. You go back and get them," I said.

Fighting against the current of the crowd, she trotted back to her classroom as Irv, Dian and I hugged the wall, trying to avoid being run down by a herd of kids leaving school on a Halloween sugar high. Selam returned, brandishing her sneakers in her hand. We advanced only a couple of feet before she said, "My coat!"

"Do you need to go back again?" I asked as I struggled to keep the frustration from my voice.

"No, I think it's in my backpack."

"Are you sure?"

She didn't answer and continued walking through the front doors.

On the phone, I reminded Selam of Friday's events.

"I thought it was in my backpack, but it wasn't. And we cleaned out my mom's car, and I looked in the lost and found, and I can't find it anywhere," Selam said in a dispirited tone.

I figured that my bubbly girl, sounding so deflated, was probably in trouble with her parents. Her tendency to lose goggles every time she went swimming had frustrated her mom, and now her winter coat was missing.

"Sorry sweetie, I don't know what happened to your coat," I said.

"OK, bye. See you Saturday." She hung up the phone without the customary small talk. Usually a phone call with Selam meant a half hour of chattering about school, her classmates or the *Junie B.* book she was reading. Today it was all business.

My heart ached. Selam's missing coat brought me back to my own childhood. I remembered the times I had been chastised when I, like Selam, frequently lost things.

"One boot? How can you lose one boot?" My father railed when I came home from junior high in a snowstorm wearing my gym shoes. "The kids were kicking it around the locker room, and it disappeared." I was terrified of where his anger might take him — just shouting or a slap today? My father fumed and fussed, pacing across the living room, shaking his head and muttering, "No common sense. That girl has no common sense."

I was grateful he used only words, but it wasn't the first — or last — time I had to come home to admit sheepishly that I had lost something. There was the transistor radio at the beach, which I had asked some boys on the adjacent blanket to watch while I went to the water's edge for a dip with my friends. There were the numerous single gloves that disappeared over the years. And worst of all was the incident when I was a preteen and dropped a comb into the window well of the car. It rattled for all the years we owned that Rambler, a constant, audible reminder of my imperfections.

Now, decades later, I tossed and turned as I tried unsuccessfully to fall asleep. My unsettled thoughts flitted between my childhood ordeals and Selam's missing jacket. I was picking at the scabs of deep-rooted sores, reopening the painful wounds of my childhood failures to meet my father's standards of responsibility.

Should I have made Selam return to her classroom or at least checked her backpack before we left school last Friday? Would this whole incident have been avoided if I had made her look for the coat right away? I perseverated.

Whose responsibility was it? Hers or mine? She's only eight. I should have followed up and not assumed the coat was in her backpack. My mind continued down the labyrinth of could haves and should haves.

Alas, Selam's coat never showed up, and she had to contribute ten dollars of the money she earned for doing chores to help buy a new jacket. Did it teach her more *achrayut*? Unfortunately, she lost the second coat just a few weeks later. And more than once she left her third coat abandoned on the playground after shedding it during recess. Luckily, the third time was the charm; she was able to retrieve that coat from the lost and found. The lesson of responsibility for her belongings was a work in progress.

While Selam, like me, was remiss when it came to possessions, we both sometimes took more than our share of *achrayut* in other aspects of our lives.

High school friends, knowing I would have it written down, called me when they forgot our algebra homework assignment. Colleagues at work did not worry about completing a newsletter because they were certain I would meet the deadline no matter how late I had to stay in the office. At Beth Evergreen, congregants could be sure I'd be the first one there to unlock the synagogue and turn on the lights for an evening program.

My family knew they could rely on me to remember doctor appointments, grocery lists and school assignments. I balanced the checkbook and the schedule. When our son, Kevin, moved back home for a short time after college, he woke up one morning and said, "Oh, I just remembered. We have a potluck at the office today. What do you have that I can bring?" One more time, I came to the rescue, mixing up a quick pasta salad.

A therapist once cautioned me. "You don't have to be the hub of your family's wheel, taking responsibility for everything in their lives." It was a hard lesson for me to learn, and now I was having another chance as a grandmother.

Selam also tended to take too much responsibility for others.

"No, we're not on that page, we're supposed to do page seventy-two," she loudly insisted to her classmates when Mrs. M. assigned them workbook pages to complete.

"Dian, you didn't brush your teeth yet. Go now," she reminded her brother, her sense of responsibility mixed with a strong dose of big sister nagging.

While Dian could be as forgetful as Selam and sometimes left a tornado in his wake after playing with his hundreds of tiny Lego pieces, he took responsibility for his school work. When I volunteered in his classroom each Tuesday, I noticed with great pride that the line beside his name on the wall chart was filled with brightly colored stickers, rewards for completing work, often surpassing most of his classmates.

His dependability was noted by his friends too. When Lee brought a treasured, well-worn Zombie comic book to school, all the boys clamored to borrow it. The glue on its spine was on the verge of disintegrating, and the book, already missing a number of pages, was at risk of losing many more. Lee lent the book to Dian.

"He said I was the only one in the class that he would trust with the book," Dian told us, gingerly turning the pages.

"How's it going?" I asked.

"So far, so good," Dian replied. Irv and I turned to each other and widely grinned.

But alas, the spine of the book gave way, more pages fell out, and the book was in shambles. Heidi purchased a replacement copy.

"It's really not fair. Lee's book was falling apart, and now he has a brand-new one," Dian said with a pout. "And I don't have one."

My heart ached for Dian. I resisted the urge to run out and buy him his own copy of the book. After all, it really wasn't his fault that the book fell apart; it was in pretty rough shape when he got it. Yet it was a fairly painless lesson in being a responsible friend.

Achrayut, like all *Mussar* traits, I reflected, is a practice in finding the right balance. So how could I find equilibrium when it came to taking responsibility for my actions and the actions of others?

It was a lesson that was hard to practice as a parent. Too often I had come to the rescue by bringing a left-behind textbook to school or helping edit an essay the night before it was due. My kids didn't have to bear the responsibility of their problems if I bore it for them.

Now I had another chance with my grandkids as teachers. If I took the blame for their actions, I wasn't being helpful. I was depriving them of the opportunity to learn from the consequences of their deeds. Selam's lost coat and Dian's tattered book had tangible costs and tough, yet valuable lessons.

I found reinforcement in the words of Vanessa Ochs, author of *Sarah Laughed*, "As much as we are loath to let a child go, we must nonetheless find safe and wise ways to launch our children into the world if they are to survive and flourish as independent, skillful and competent people."

So next time, I promised myself, rather than fret over the grandchildren's losses, I would try to welcome them as a way to practice the *middah* of *achrayut*.

Journal prompts
- Are you more likely to take too much or too little responsibility? Why?
- What causes you to take too much responsibility, leading to stress?
- When have you failed to take responsibility for your words or actions? What was the result?

Joy — *Simcha*

"Joy is the inner feeling that emerges from an openhearted connection with another or others in which the barriers of separation are dissolved. Happiness may not be an attainable goal because our wants are insatiable and their satisfaction transitory but because we really can connect to other people, joy is entirely within our reach."

— Alan Morinis

When the shrill sound of the alarm woke me, I jumped out of bed, eager to make Dian's almond flour birthday cake with chocolate cream cheese filling. I had never tried this recipe, and I was fretting about how it would turn out. I wanted the cake to be perfect for Dian's eighth birthday. As I placed the batter-filled metal pans into the oven, the early morning sun streamed through the kitchen window.

By the time I had finished baking the cake and frosting it, the fickle February weather had changed. The sun had vanished, replaced by ominous gray clouds. Soon large, heavy snowflakes covered the driveway, and the road in front of our house turned icy white.

The storm intensified as I waited for Heidi to pick me up and take me to the bowling alley where we'd meet Dian's friends for the party. I paced back and forth in front of the living room window. She was fifteen minutes late, and I was trying to control my worry. *Where are they? I hope the highway isn't too slick. Should I call her cell phone? No, I don't want her distracted by a ringing phone in these conditions.* My mind danced feverishly as I kept peering down the road, worry overtaking my anticipated joy of celebrating with my grandkids.

I came upon worry honestly; it was part of my genetic code. My parents and their parents before them were worriers. My grandparents had escaped persecution by fleeing from Russia. They had learned to be wary in a world where danger lurked around every corner. And though they had tried to absorb the immigrant dream of a safe America, they never completely lost their fear. Instead, they passed it on to the next generation, my parents.

As a teen, if I arrived home just a few minutes after curfew, I was greeted by my mother, sitting on the couch in the dark. "Where were you?" Her voice trembled, overwrought with a lifetime of pent-up anxiety. Rather than asking what movie I had seen, she fretted about why I was late.

Worrying was as natural as breathing to me too. When I returned home after a day at the beach, I expected to see my parents in their customary seats on the living room couch in front of the TV. The room was empty. My stomach clutched as I climbed the first three steps toward their bedroom and shouted, "Are you here? What's wrong?" My parents had just been upstairs changing their clothes for a night out, but for that moment I feared some horrible tragedy had befallen our family. I lived under the looming cloud of some unforeseen event that would sever the loving connection; it was a habitual barrier to joy.

So when Heidi's white van finally turned into the driveway, I felt my shoulders drop. The sight of my daughter and the grandkids, safe and sound, transformed my worry to gratitude. I pulled on my coat, hat and gloves, kissed Irv goodbye and trudged out into the rapidly accumulating snow, carefully balancing a bag of gifts and the home-made birthday cake.

As I settled in the front seat, I peered over my shoulder to glance at Selam and Dian, buckled in their car seats and filled with energy as they anticipated their time at the bowling alley.

By now, Selam had been in our family for more than six years, Dian more than five. And every time I heard their voices on the phone, their car appeared on our road or I walked into their classrooms, my heart filled with a sense of well-being, a sense of *simcha* like no other. My connection to them couldn't have been any deeper if they had been born of my own blood. I cherished every moment in their presence.

After a painstakingly slow drive down the icy highway, the kids couldn't wait to escape from the car and greet Dian's waiting friends. Entering the warmth of the bowling alley, they peeled off their coats and gloves and stood on tiptoes, peering over the counter and ordering bowling shoes. Marveling at the multitude of multi-colored choices, they raced to the stacks of bowling bowls.

"Does the speckled red or the neon green fit your hand better? How does your thumb feel?" I asked Selam. "Is that green one too heavy?"

When Selam, Dian and his friends had chosen their favorites, we went to the last lane in the alley and lined up the rainbow of balls. Each child entered his name on the computer to record the scores.

Bowling alleys have sure changed since the days I was a teen when most of my balls wound up in the gutter, I thought as I gazed at the modern technology. The staff had set up lane guards adjacent to the gutters, so the kids could knock down at least one pin every time.

When I had bowled with my friends in the 1960s, we had calculated the score in our heads and filled out paper score sheets with stubby wooden pencils. Today, the kids saw their scores appear magically on a digital screen overhead.

"Look, I got them all down." Dian's friend Luke jumped up and down as his numbers appeared on the screen. Selam cheered when seven of her pins went down and sharing in her joy, I gave her a hug.

The kids gobbled pizza, chicken fingers and fries between taking turns bowling and plugging tokens into the ear-piercing video games in the adjacent room. Finally it was time for Dian to blow out the candles and share the cake that I had made early that morning.

"Thank you, Moo. This is exactly what I wanted," Dian affirmed between bites.

Satiated with food and the joy of celebration, we said goodbye to Dian's friends, turned in the bowling shoes and headed for the car.

"I loved my party. It was the best ever," Dian exclaimed as we trudged through the accumulating snow.

Like the black pavement hidden under the white snow, for that moment the darkness of my worrying was buried under the light of shared joy.

— ❤ —

A few weeks later, on a warm winter day with most of the snow melted, we decided to take a hike in the woods. Dian stopped every few feet to admire and gather an assortment of pinkish-orange granite stones freckled with pockets of white and black mineral deposits.

"Look at this one, Moo! It has shiny black speckles on the side. Put it in my pack, please!" Dian exclaimed as he reached down for yet another treasure.

"Isn't your pack getting heavy with all those rocks? Are you sure you want more?"

"It's just making me stronger. I want them."

Then he stopped abruptly at a large flat rock, its edges jutting into the trail. Coral-colored with pencil-thin lines of black, the rock had a long, pointed streak of white quartz down its center. Dian knelt and ran his finger over the milky-colored stripe.

"See this, Moo. It's a sword left here by the first boy angel. If I rub it, it will protect my family. Did you know there are boy and girl angels?"

I had walked the trail countless times and had never been drawn to this apparently very special rock. Seeing the world through Dian's eyes, the commonplace became exciting, wondrous and even magical.

Selam, too, spent the walk in an enchanted place inside her imagination. As we hiked side-by-side up the steep trail, Selam chatted about a flying machine she was going to invent. Made of metal, plastic and wood, the machine would be powered by four huge fans. It would take us to Disney World, but wouldn't fly too high, so we could stick our heads out the big window and enjoy the fresh air and the scenery. The interior of the flying machine would be decorated with murals of princesses, lit by a huge, sparkly chandelier in the center.

On the way down the trail, Selam and Heidi fell behind. Dian and I arrived back at the car and shared a snack while we waited. Another car pulled beside us, and two older men emerged.

"Is this a trailhead?" one asked.

I answered with an enthusiastic "yes," describing how the trail went up the hill alongside the stream.

"Thank you," the man said flatly as he and his companion plodded onto the trail.

"They didn't seem very excited. Maybe because they are so old," Dian commented after the two left.

"I'm old, and I'm excited about hiking."

"That's because you hike with kids," Dian replied. He was right. Through his eyes, the ordinary became extraordinary. Every step was an adventure.

Finally Heidi and Selam emerged from the woods, their arms overflowing with fallen tree branches.

"We're going to use the sticks to start building my flying machine," Selam enthused as she piled the dead wood into the back of my car.

Though the hike had involved a long, uphill climb, the kids were full of energy on the short drive back to their house.

"I'm going to start building my plane this afternoon. Will you help me, Mom?" Selam asked.

"I have lots of rocks to put on my dresser. I'll arrange them by size. No, by color," Dian announced.

They eagerly removed their treasures from my car, and exhausted, I decided to head straight home. Later that afternoon, I went back to the car to unload my hiking boots and backpack. I noticed that my supplies were covered by an abundance of souvenirs from our hike — slivers of tree bark, pine needles and a few forgotten stones.

In the past, I would have fretted about the detritus requiring a vacuum to make my car fit for adult passengers. Today I smiled at the tangible reminders of the wonders of hiking with my grandchildren. My heart was filled with *simcha* as I reflected on the deep connections I had developed with Selam and Dian, with nature, with what is and what could be.

Journal prompts

- How do connections to others bring you joy?
- What are your obstacles to joy?
- How do you overcome the obstacles?

Gratitude — *Hakarat Ha'tov*

"Gratitude rejoices with her sister joy and is always ready to light a candle and have a party."

— Rebbe Nachman of Breslov

Arriving home after a fun-filled Friday, the grandkids dashed into the kitchen to greet their dad. Irv and I lagged behind, Irv to pet the dog and I to gather forgotten sweatshirts, water bottles and aluminum tins filled with lunch leftovers.

As we entered the house, I overheard their animated voices recounting our day together.

"We went to three places today," Selam exclaimed. "First swimming; then out to eat in the mac and cheese restaurant."

"A mac and cheese restaurant?" Robin asked.

"It's a small wood building. You go inside and stand at the counter and order mac and cheese with lots of different stuff in it," Dian interjected. "They had bags of chips too. "

"After lunch we went to the park, and we tossed rocks and sticks in the river. And we watched the rocks sink and the sticks float away," Selam finished.

"Sounds like you had fun. Did you say thank you to Moo and Poo?" Robin asked.

"Thank you, Moo and Poo," the grandkids said in stilted harmony.

The obligatory thank you was an important lesson in manners, yet I had already felt their gratitude in their enthusiastic retelling of our day. It had reminded me how grateful I was for our adventure-filled

Fridays. I was receiving more than I was giving.

"You are welcome. Thank you for a special day. We wouldn't have gone to such fun places without you. My curry-spiced mac and cheese was delicious! And Poo and I loved guessing which branch would float fastest down the river," I responded.

Feeling *hakarat ha'tov* had come naturally during the big moments in my life — when Selam finally arrived in America, when my children graduated from college, when I published a book. But before grand-kids, I often had trouble remembering to be grateful for the small gifts of everyday life. In general, I was more likely to focus on what could go wrong than appreciate what was going well.

The words in *The Book of Joy* accurately reflected my experience: "Scientists have long known that our brains evolved with a negative bias. . . Gratitude cuts across this default mode of the mind. It allows us to see what is good and right, and not just what is bad and wrong."

My grandkids are teaching me gratitude in the day-to-day goodness of life. Could I find gratitude in what felt like challenging situations?

A few days later, I had the chance to find out when I woke up to a driveway buried in snow. *Oh no! I've got to get out there and shov-el so I can get to my committee meeting. Would the snow be heavy? How many inches and how long would it take?* I fretted, dreading the task, as I donned my fleece-lined boots, purple-fringed ski cap and bulky gloves before heading outside.

Picking up the snow shovel, I faced a *bechirah* point. Could I mind-fully choose gratitude in this unwelcome early morning chore? By in-tentionally looking for opportunities to be grateful, I found them.

After a few minutes of tossing heavy piles of snow off the driveway, I stopped to catch my breath. I looked around and observed the beau-ty of a Colorado morning after a snowstorm — the bright sun in the cloudless, turquoise sky; the crisp, clean air; the sparkle of the snow-tipped trees. *How lucky I am to live in nature*, I thought. Soon another opportunity for gratitude came in the form of a helper.

"Hi Dan." With a sense of relief, I greeted my 70-year-old neighbor as he walked across the icy street with his shovel. Together we tackled the mountain of hard-packed snow left by the county plow at the edge of my driveway.

"I was really dreading lifting this 'cement' by myself. Thanks so much for your help. I know you already spent an hour working on your own driveway," I said.

My shoveling became a successful experiment in discovering and expressing gratitude in a mundane chore. As Rabbi Amy Eilberg wrote in *Yashar*, The Mussar Institute newsletter, "Without question, expression of gratitude is fundamental to a relationship. A steady diet of negative comments is lethal, while words of appreciation make love and kindness grow all around us."

Expanding my *Mussar* practice, I challenged myself to go one more step. *Could I find a "blessing in disguise" and experience hakarat ha'tov for a scary event in our lives?*

I recalled the cold winter night when I was reading in front of the fire, already in my pajamas. It was less than two months after Dian had joined our family. The harsh sound of the phone interrupted the peaceful silence.

"Dian has a fever of 104. I'm driving to urgent care. Can you find an open pharmacy if I need to fill a prescription?" Heidi asked, her trembling voice revealing fear.

"Yes, and I'll come with you. Meet me at the Kum & Go."

Dressing quickly, I rushed to the gas station and jumped out of my car and into Heidi's. We sped down the mountain as two-year-old Dian, flushed with fever, whimpered in the backseat.

"There it is," I pointed.

Heidi swerved into the parking lot, turned off the car and unbuckled Dian, his dark, straight hair slick with sweat. She carried him into the dimly lit building and opened the door to the medical office where several other families with sick kids waited in uneasy silence. As we got ready to sit down, Dian's body went stiff and started convulsing.

"Something's not right with my boy," Heidi shouted.

The nurse hurried us into the back room, where the doctor placed Dian on his side and held him until the seizure stopped. They called for an ambulance to transport Dian to the nearest hospital. Heidi accompanied him while I followed in her Volkswagen, struggling to remember how to drive a manual transmission.

I raced into the emergency room and found my family. Dian had been given ibuprofen to fight the fever, and huge welts began popping up all over his forehead and skull. *Was it some strange disease he had brought from China? An allergic reaction?* Heidi and I looked on in horror as the doctor examined him.

"We'd better keep him overnight," the doctor announced.

The next couple of hours passed in a blur of fear and worry as the medical team conducted tests and settled him in a hospital bed. At midnight, I jerked the Volkswagen up the highway homeward while Heidi remained at Dian's side.

After a fitful night of sleep, I drove back to the hospital with fresh clothes for Heidi and Dian. Anxious about what I would find, I hesitantly stepped into the antiseptic room. No one was there. Then I heard the comforting sound of my daughter's voice coming from the bathroom, where she was bathing Dian. The bumps on his head had shrunk; the fever was gone; and Dian's bright spirit had returned.

"He had a febrile seizure, not uncommon in young children. He'll outgrow it by the time he is five," the doctor consoled. "The bumps were probably a reaction to the fever or to the medication. Don't give him ibuprofen to play it safe. Use Tylenol as soon as he starts to have a fever, so it doesn't get too high. That will prevent the seizures. You can take him home now."

Over the next several years, we watched Dian carefully. I kept a thermometer, Benadryl and children's Tylenol at the ready. If his temperature rose when he visited us, I immediately called his parents and provided the suggested treatment. Keeping his fevers under control worked; Dian never suffered another febrile seizure. I breathed a deep sigh of relief when he turned five.

Reflecting on the crisis years later, I saw it as an opportunity for *hakarat ha'tov* on several levels. Most immediate was the gratitude for Dian's quick recovery without any lasting ill effects. As time passed, I felt grateful that the seizures didn't recur, and for the most part he was a healthy child. As gratitude researcher Robert Emmons says, "Trials and suffering can actually refine and deepen gratefulness if we allow them to show us not to take things for granted."

And finally, I was struck with gratitude for a possibility I hadn't considered before. *Perhaps it wasn't his first attack,* I thought. *Maybe Dian had experienced a febrile seizure in rural China. How scary that would have been for his parents, who lacked both understanding of what was happening and access to immediate medical care. They would have had no way of knowing it was a temporary condition that was easily treated and preventable. Was that the impetus for their courageous act of leaving him in front of a hospital where he could get help?*

Looking through my *Mussar* lens, Dian's seizure became a blessing in disguise as well as a plausible explanation of his parents' sacrifice. By abandoning him, they provided him with better access to health care — and gave us an incredible gift.

I was learning that the soul trait of *hakarat ha'tov* is all about perspective. With mindful practice and help from Dian and Selam, I could experience gratitude not only for the everyday blessings, but also for events that at first blush appeared to be challenges.

Journal prompts
- What triggered your gratitude today?
- What gets in the way of feeling grateful?
- When have you experienced a blessing in disguise?

Your Love Is Blasting in My Heart

My *Mussar* journey began several years before my adopted grand-children, Selam and Dian, arrived in my life. Some days I felt good about my progress in showing more compassion, patience and honor. At other times I was frustrated by my backsliding as I reacted with a lack of grace or kindness.

When my grandchildren, two treasured gifts from around the globe, became part of our family, I found not only renewed motivation, but also new teachers. My *Mussar* practice grew exponentially through my grandchildren's intentional and unintended lessons. They have taught me that the opportunities for growth never stop. I agree with Greg Marcus, who wrote, "The only graduation from your spiritual curriculum is death. I'm in no hurry to get there."

I have come to believe that every human being is on a soul journey. When I acknowledge and embrace my journey, I can make meaningful choices for the betterment of the world in which I live, whether merely in my own family or for the greater good of humanity. It's simple and difficult at the same time. It requires me to be mindful as I face every-day situations and interactions: Will I have a knee-jerk reaction to a stimulus or will I respond in a way that is respectful of others as well as myself?

I find inspiration in these letters from Dian and Selam. Their notes hang on the side of my refrigerator, a daily reminder of love, gratitude and why I seek to become a better person.

My hope is that you, dear reader, find a source of inspiration as compelling for your soul growth as I have found in my grandchildren. Thank you for accompanying me on this journey.

Letter from a first grader

Dear Moo,

You are the best gramma becuz you take us to plasis. I like wen you play with us. Thank you for coming to school on Tuesday.

Love,
Dian

Letter from a third grader

Dear funest grandma,

You are a spectacelor fun grandma! You bring us on amazing adventures. You give us many, many freedoms. Such as, go places like elishes, Jump Street, Big Time, parks! Your love for me is blasting in my heart! I love you so!

Sinserely,
Selamnesh

Glossary of Hebrew Terms

Note: There are numerous variations of how these words are trans-literated and pronounced in English. In most cases, the words below offer the Sephardic pronunciation as in Modern Hebrew. "Ch" or "kh" is pronounced as in the name Bach.

Mussar (moo-SAR) – discipline, a Jewish spiritual and ethical practice to grow one's soul in the service of others

Middah (mee-DAH) (plural, *middot* – mee-DOET) – measure, soul trait, virtue, value, measurable quality of character

The *middot* featured in this book:

Achrayut (ach--rye-YOOT) – responsibility

Ametz lev (ah-METZ-lehv) – courage of the heart

Anavah (ah-nah-VAH) – humility

Bitachon (bit-ach-OWN) – trust

Emet (EM- et) – truth

Hakarat ha'tov (ha-kah-RAHT ha-TOV) – gratitude, recognizing the good

Hitlamdut (heet-lahm-DOOT) – awe, curiosity, openness to learning

Nedivut (ne-dee-VOOT) – generosity

Rachamim (rach-ah-MEEM) – compassion

Savlanut (sahv-lah-NEWT) – patience

Simcha (seem-CHA) – joy

Zehirut (zeh-hee-ROOT) – mindfulness

Zerizut (zeh-ree-ZOOT) – enthusiasm

Other Hebrew words used in this book:

Bechirah (b'chee-RAH) – choice

Bema (BEE-mah) – the podium or platform in the synagogue

Chesbon hanefesh (chesh-BONE-ha-NE-fesh) – accounting of the soul for spiritual growth

Dreidel (DRAY-dull) – the four-sided spinning top children play with at Chanukah

L'dor vador (lah-DOOR vah-DOOR) – (transmitting values) from one generation to the next

Menorah (men-oh-RAH) – the candelabra used at Chanukah

Seder (SAY-der) – Passover celebration that includes reading the Exodus story and serving traditional foods to commemorate our freedom from slavery

Shabbat (sha-BAHT) – Sabbath, the weekly holiday beginning just before sunset on Friday evening and lasting until nightfall on Saturday

Taschlich (tash-LEEKH) – custom of throwing bread crumbs into moving water at the High Holy Days, symbolizing casting off sins

Va'ad (v'AHD) – orally sharing *Mussar* personal successes and challenges with a partner or small group in a confidential setting to enhance accountability, reflection and self-awareness

Resources

Lama, Dalai and Tutu, Desmond with Abrams, Jacob. *The Book of Joy.* New York: Avery, Penguin Random House, 2016.

Eilberg, Rabbi Amy. Website: www.rabbiamyeilberg.com

Emmons, Robert. *Gratitude Works!* San Francisco: Josey-Bass, 2013.

Feinsmith, Rabbi Sam (2014, Sept. 1), *The Blessing of Curiosity, Sh'ma, A Journal of Jewish Ideas,* Retrieved from http://shma.com/2014/09/the-blessing-of-curiosity/

Fuchs-Kreimer, Rabbi Nancy. *Parenting as a Spiritual Journey.* Woodstock, Vermont: Jewish Lights Publishing, 1996.

Gold, Rabbi Shefa. *Modeh, Ani: Beginning the Day with Gratitude.* https://www.myjewishlearning.com/article/modeh-ani-beginning-the-day-with-gratitude
Also see: www.rabbishefagold.com

Jaffe, Rabbi David. *Changing the World from the Inside Out.* Boulder, Colorado: Trumpeter, 2016.

Korngold, Rabbi Jamie. *The God Upgrade: Finding Your 21st Century Spirituality in Judaism's 5,000-Year-Old Tradition.* Woodstock, Vermont: Jewish Lights, 2011.

Marcus, Greg. *The Spiritual Practice of Good Actions: Finding Balance Through the Soul Traits of Mussar.* Woodbury, Minnesota: Llewellyn Publications, 2016.

Morinis, Alan. *Everyday Holiness.* Boston: Trumpeter Press, 2007.

_____. *Everyday Holy Day*. Boulder: Trumpeter Press, 2010

_____. *With Heart in Mind*. Boston: Trumpeter Press, 2014.

_____. *Climbing Jacob's Ladder*. New York: Broadway Books, 2002.

Ochs, Vanessa L. *Sarah Laughed*. New York: McGraw-Hill, 2004.

Sacks, Rabbi Jonathan, *When Is It Permitted to Tell A Lie?*, Retrieved from https://www.chabad.org/parshah/article_cdo/aid/2759422/jewish/When-Is-It-Permitted-to-Tell-a-Lie.htm

Salzberg, Sharon. *Faith*. New York: Riverhead Books, 2002. Website: https://www.sharonsalzberg.com/

Schwartz, Rabbi Itamar. *Getting to Know Your Soul*. Jerusalem: Bilvavi Books: 2010.

Shapiro, Rabbi Rami. *The Sacred Art of Lovingkindness: Preparing to Practice*. Woodstock,Vermont: SkyLight Paths Publishing, 2006

Stone, Ira. *A Responsible Life, The Spiritual Path of Mussar*. New York: Aviv Press, 2006.

Telushkin, Rabbi Joseph. *The Book of Jewish Values*. New York: Bell Tower, 2000.

Weinberg, Rabbi Sheila Peltz. *Surprisingly Happy: An Atypical Religious Memoir*. Amherst, MA: White River Press, 2010.

Zeitlin, Rabbi Harry, blog, https://rabbizeitlin.com/

Pirkei Avot: Ethics of Our Fathers, part of the Mishnah, the first text of Jewish oral law

Introductory Chapter Quotes

"When we fully set our heart on doing something, our determination can give us the inner strength to overcome fear, doubt and other obstacles in our path." Rabbi Barry Schwartz, author and director of The Jewish Publication Society, Philadelphia

"The only thing happening is this present moment, which is going so fast that we have almost lost it before it is even here." Jetsunma Tenzin Palmo, author, teacher, founding director of Dongyu Gatsal Ling Nunnery, India

"The essence of patience is to live in the present. We are impatient because we want to be in the future faster than reality will take us there." Rabbi Zelig Pliskin, Orthodox rabbi, psychologist and author

"To curiosity we can credit the survival and expansion of our species, our sciences, and our faith. It holds the key to unlocking wonderment, to transforming the 'same-old, same-old syndrome' to something new and bold." Rabbi Jamie Arnold, Congregation Beth Evergreen, Evergreen, Colorado

"If you see a person giving liberally, it means his wealth will grow; if you see one who shuns charity, it means his wealth will dwindle." Midrash Mishle, rabbinic commentary on the Book of Proverbs

"In the long run, we shape our lives, and we shape ourselves. The process never ends until we die. And the choices we make are ultimately our own responsibility." Eleanor Roosevelt, 1884-1962, diplomat and longest-serving first lady of the United States

"The goal of Trust is to let go of worry and control, to learn that whatever happens, you will be able to deal with it." Greg Marcus, author (See Resources)

"The word "enthusiasm" comes from the Greek word "entheos" which means the God within. And the happiest, most interesting people are those who have found the secret of maintaining their enthusiasm, that God within." Earl Nightingale, 1921-1989, American radio host and motivational author

"Compassion is to sense another person's existence, understand his thinking and feelings, connect to him, and to realize that the connection itself is the goal." Rabbi Itamar Schwartz, author (See Resources)

"Before you tell a truth that can cause only pain and inflict gratuitous hurt, ask yourself why you should tell it. There are indeed times when a pretty lie is preferable to an ugly truth." Rabbi Joseph Telushkin, spiritual leader, scholar and author (See Resources)

"The practice of humility requires us to view each person we encounter as our teacher and to struggle to learn something from each person." Rabbi Ira Stone, author and leading figure in the modern *Mussar* movement (See Resources)

"Joy is the inner feeling that emerges from an openhearted connection with another or others in which the barriers of separation are dissolved. Happiness may not be an attainable goal because our wants are insatiable and their satisfaction transitory but because we really can connect to other people, joy is entirely within our reach." Alan Morinis, founder of The Mussar Institute and author (See Resources)

"Gratitude rejoices with her sister joy and is always ready to light a candle and have a party." Rebbe Nachman of Breslov, (1772-1810), a master of Chassidut, the Jewish movement founded by his great-grandfather, the Baal Shem Tov

Acknowledgments

My book would not have been possible without Rabbi Jamie Arnold, whose wisdom and decade-long *Mussar* class at Congregation Beth Evergreen kept me learning, practicing and growing. I owe much gratitude to my *Mussar* study groups who supported and encouraged me.

Deep thanks to Alan Morinis, whose book *Everyday Holiness* became my go-to resource and whose visit to Beth Evergreen served as a catalyst for a life-changing journey. I found ongoing inspiration from his writings on The Mussar Institute website.

David Jaffe's *Tikkun Middot Project* curriculum and teachings at the Institute for Jewish Spirituality and Beth Evergreen, as well as his book, *Changing the World from the Inside Out*, provided deeper understanding of *Mussar*, helping me improve my practice.

My writing became infinitely better with the help of Hearthfire Writers Group, Rabbi Jamie Arnold, Diane Mott Davidson, Amy Frykholm and Joanne Greenberg. Members of Colorado Press Women Writers Group, Judi Buehrer, Nancy Bierman, Donna Bryson, Dala Giffin, Mart Kelle, Ann Lockhart, Marilyn Hosea and Sandy Nance, offered suggestions and encouragement. To Gay Porter DeNileon, Teresa Ford and Kathy Ireland, thank you for your eagle-eyed editing and insightful critique.

I am eternally grateful to my biggest fan and supporter, my husband, Irv, who encouraged my writing and all other endeavors I've pursued. My children, Heidi and Kevin, and grandchildren, Selam and Dian, provided the inspiration and stories for this book.

About the Author

Marilyn Saltzman has studied *Mussar* for more than a decade. She has served as a *Mussar* facilitator at Congregation Beth Evergreen, Evergreen, Colorado, after receiving training at the Institute for Jewish Spirituality. She was president of the Board of Directors and chair of the Adult Education Committee at Beth Evergreen.

Marilyn is the co-author of several nonfiction books, the award-winning *Building School Communities, Strategies for Leaders* and *Reflections, Learning by Doing* with BJ Meadows; *Maybe Tomorrow, A Hidden Child of the Holocaust* with Eric Cahn; and *Dave Sanders, Columbine Teacher, Coach, Hero* with Linda Sanders. She wrote a chapter in *Reclaiming School in the Aftermath of Trauma*, which received the 2013 Colorado Book Award, Anthology. She holds a bachelor of arts from Brooklyn College and a master of business administration from the University of Colorado Denver.

Marilyn worked as public relations manager for Jefferson County Public Schools, Colorado, for twenty years and has been a public relations consultant for school districts and education associations across the nation. She is the proud grandmother of Selamnesh Faith and Dian Le Dusharm.